CB Radio

QUESTIONS & ANSWERS

CB Radio

F. C. Judd G2BCX

Newnes Technical Books

Newnes Technical Books

is an imprint of the Butterworth Group

which has principal offices in

London, Boston, Durban, Singapore, Sydney, Toronto, Wellington

First published 1982

© Butterworth & Co. (Publishers) Ltd, 1982

British Library Cataloguing in Publication Data

Judd, F. C.
  CB radio. – (Questions and answers)
  1. Citizens band radio – Great Britain
  I. Title
  621.3845'4'0941   TK6570.C5

  ISBN 0-408-01216-1

Photoset by Butterworths Litho Preparation Department
Printed in England by Whitstable Litho Ltd, Whitstable, Kent

Preface

Since the invention of wireless telegraphy about 1900 'radio' has been continuously developed to become the most important and most used method of world wide communication.

Two-way communication by radio is in itself a fascinating subject and for many years radio amateurs (hams) have been allocated special frequency bands for their hobby. However, a licence to use the amateur radio bands can only be obtained after passing an examination designed to show that the amateur understands how his equipment works. For some of the amateur radio bands it is also necessary to pass a morse code test at 12 words per minute.

Radio channels for more or less unrestricted short-range two-way communication by people without any technical knowledge were made available under licence to citizens of the USA about 30 years ago and the band of frequencies allocated became known as 'Citizens' Band'. Only in recent years has a similar facility been made available to citizens of other countries and finally to those in Great Britain. Citizens' Band radio became legal in the UK on 2 November 1981. It is exclusively for public use under licence authorised by the Home Office, the responsible body in the UK for all radio communications frequencies and purposes.

For those who wish to obtain a licence and take up CB radio, many questions arise concerning the necessary equipment and its operation. The aim of this book is to provide answers to those questions as concisely as possible.

F.C.J.

Contents

1 Introduction to CB Radio 1

2 Technical matters 11

3 Equipment for CB Radio 34

4 Antennas and radio propagation at 27 MHz and 934 MHz 53

5 Operating procedures 71

6 Glossary of technical terms 91

Index 101

1
Introduction to CB radio

What is Citizens' Band radio?

It is a short-range two-way radio service for use by anyone holding a Citizens' Band Radio licence. CB radio is intended for communicating with other people either from necessity or for general interest and can be regarded as a hobby similar to amateur radio but without the restrictions imposed by the amateur radio licence. Broadcasting or advertising are not allowed, neither is the transmission of music.

CB radio began in the USA because of public demand for an otherwise 'free' means of communication with as little restriction, technical or otherwise, as possible. Its use in other countries, now including the UK, is on much the same basis.

What has CB radio to offer?

A great deal provided it is used responsibly. It offers considerable social activity as there are many clubs and other organisations catering for CB operators. It is a means of keeping in touch with others without the need to write or use the telephone, and a way of making new friends. As its uses are almost unrestricted, CB radio can be used for passing messages in cases of emergency, giving road traffic reports to others, requesting help in case of breakdown on the road, obtaining the services of fire, ambulance or Police in cases of accidents and when remote from a telephone.

It is a vital link with the outside world for elderly or infirm people, especially those living alone and without access to a telephone or near neighbour. It can be used for business purposes, for keeping in touch with employees away from the office, although it cannot be used for advertising. There is no age limit and no restrictions as far as family use is concerned. A CB station can be at home or in a car, a boat or any public vehicle. The only exception is that *CB radio must not be used in any aircraft.*

Do many people use CB?

Even before CB was made legal in the UK it was used by thousands of operators (illegally). Over 152 000 licences were issued in the first three months after legalisation and at the time of writing the number was increasing at the rate of 9000 per month. Not everyone is operating at the same time although the allocated band is often very crowded. The working range of a CB radio system is limited but separation by distance enables a number of operators to use the same channel simultaneously. At times the bands are very busy, particularly outside business hours, i.e. at weekends and in the evenings. There are however, periods when only very short range working is possible because of interference from continental CB stations, many of whom use high transmitting powers. This applies only to the 27 MHZ band, which is in general use for CB in other countries, including all the near European countries.

How is the working range of a CB station limited?

By restricting the amount of transmitter power that may be fed to the antenna and by restrictions on the types of antenna that may be used. More details appear in the answers to later questions.

What is the working range?

Maximum operating range depends on the terrain: for the 27 MHz band up to 13–16 km (8–10 miles) in open country, and up to 5–6 km (3 or 4 miles) in towns. For the 934 MHz band,

2

16–20 km (10–12 miles) in open country and about 3–5 km (2 or 3 miles) in towns. Somewhat greater distances may be possible between two base stations and less from mobile to mobile. The capture effect (see Chapter 2) also provides a limitation on range.

What are the CB radio bands?

The 27 MHz band has already been mentioned and is the most popular for general use. The other allocation for the UK is the 934 MHz band. The 27 MHz band, or rather the section that has been made legal in the UK, is spread over a frequency range from 27.60125 to 27.99125 MHz (the wavelength is about 11 metres) and is in what is normally regarded as the high frequency part of the radio spectrum, sometimes referred to as the 'short waves'. The 934 MHz band comes within the ultra high frequency region (UHF) (wavelength about 32 centimetres) and this is considered as being 'ultra short wave'. The actual frequency allocation is 934.025 to 934.975 MHz. Both bands are divided into a number of channels each with its own specific spot frequency, details of which are given later.

What kind of equipment is used for CB?

Typical sets are transceivers (combined transmitter/receiver) which for base station operation are normally mains powered and therefore suitable for home or office use. Transceivers used for mobile operation are similar to base stations except that they operate directly from the vehicle 12 V battery. Such sets can, however, be operated as base stations by using a mains power unit to supply 12 V. Other sets are handheld portables or walkie-talkies, which are low powered sets normally operated from internal dry (or rechargeable) batteries. All sets used for the UK CB radio service must carry the mark of compliance with performance specification.

Who is allowed to use CB?

Anyone who holds a licence and has equipment that meets the Home Office performance specifications and which is used according to the licence conditions. The licence also covers anyone who lives or is temporarily residing at the licensee's home, employees of the licensee using sets in connection with his business and anyone who hires sets from a licensee for a period of not more than 28 days. There is no limit for business use and companies who wish to use CB for office to site, or shop to van communication, for instance, are free to do so provided licences are obtained for the number of sets in use.

How is a CB licence obtained?

Licences can be purchased over the counter at all main Post Offices. Blank licence application (Fig. 1) forms are also generally included with CB equipment purchased from dealers. The licence is form completed and handed to the Post Office clerk together with the licence fee – £10 for 3 sets. You may obtain a licence for extra sets (in units of 3 for £10) up to a maximum of 15 sets. Applications for more than 15 sets must be made by post to the CB Licensing Unit, Chetwynd House, Chesterfield, Derbyshire S49 1PF, enclosing the application form and the remittance. The licence covers use on both 27 MHz and 934 MHz bands.

The licence states quite clearly who can operate sets under licence and includes details about the conditions of use, the permitted types of transmission and specified forms of antenna. The licence also shows examples of the Home Office marks of compliance that all sets for legal operation must carry on the front panel (Fig. 2). Note that 27 MHz amplitude modulated (AM) sets, including those with single sideband modulation (SSB) at present in use, are not legal because they operate on channels that are not allocated in the UK for CB radio and the sets generally do not conform to the Home Office specifications regarding interference.

4

CITIZENS' BAND RADIO LICENCE

FOR OFFICIAL USE ONLY

Expires with Last Day of | Month | Year

For on Issue f

WIRELESS TELEGRAPHY ACT 1949

How many sets do you need this licence to cover?
(Place a tick in the appropriate box)

Up to 3 | 6 | 9 | 12 | 15 | More than 15 state number above

Licence Number: 00437225

Initials of forenames: MR MS

If this is a renewal licence place a tick here

Surname:

Full Postal Address:

Postcode:

TO NOTIFY CHANGE OF NAME OR ADDRESS PLEASE TAKE THIS LICENCE TO ANY POST OFFICE FOR AMENDMENT

Licence Fee Stamps to be stuck in this column

(Each fee stamp covers up to 3 sets)

(hereinafter called the Licensee) is hereby licensed subject to the terms, provisions and limitations set out below and in the Schedule to establish and use up to ‡ ...... wireless telegraphy sending and receiving station for wireless telegraphy using only apparatus which conforms in all respects to Home Office specifications

MPT 1320 and/or MPT 1321† provided that the licensee is hereby licensed, subject as aforesaid, to establish and use one or more such stations in addition to the number of such stations specified above at any time prior to the date on which a renewal fee in respect of this licence is paid. This licence is subject to Clause 10 below, continue in force up to and including the date on which it may be duly revoked and thereafter so long as the licensee pays to the Secretary of State in advance in each year on or before that date such renewal fee as is prescribed by regulations made under Section 2(1) of the Wireless Telegraphy Act 1949

Issued on behalf of the Secretary of State for the Home Department _____

‡ To be completed by the Post Office   † To see Note overleaf

CB01 MISC 406 370324

Fig. 1. The Home Office licence for CB radio on 27 MHz and 934 MHz. Available from any main Post Office

5

Can sets designed for 27 MHz AM and SSB be legalised?

CB sets using amplitude modulation mostly operate on different frequencies (26.9 to 27.5 MHz) and because of this are illegal in the UK. It is possible that they may be capable of modification to

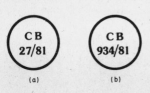

(a) (b)

Fig. 2. All CB radio transceivers that meet the Home Office specification for performance requirements as laid down in MPT1320 (27 MHz) must carry the label as shown in (a). For compliance with MPT1321 (934 MHz) the label is that shown as (b)

allow them to be operated legally and a number of firms will carry out the necessary modifications. Many of them will also collect the Customs and Excise duty if this has not already been paid. This only applies, of course, if the sets were manufactured outside the UK.

What restrictions apply to the use of CB?

There are very few restrictions – only the allocated channels may be used (see Chapter 2); only plain speech may be used (except for special digital signals designed to identify the transmitter or to activate a receiver) – there seems to be no reason why you should not speak French or Chinese, as long as it is not in code. Only angle modulation may be used (see Chapter 2); the transmitter output power must not exceed 4 W; the antenna must be of a specified type; the equipment must not cause undue interference to other radio or television equipment (more details in Chapter 2).

Do you need any technical knowledge?

Generally speaking no, although some is advisable even if only to ensure that you understand the basic functions of the equipment and to be sure that when connected it is operating correctly and not causing interference to other services or to a neighbour's radio or television. Knowledge of how to carry out repairs is not necessary because without special testing equipment anything other than a simple job of replacing a blown fuse or repairing a broken plug connection etc, would be difficult or even impossible to carry out.

How much does a CB system cost?

There are really two systems available, one for 'base station' or home use, the other for 'mobile' use on a motor vehicle or boat etc. Most transceivers for base station operation are mains powered and prices range from about £80 to £200 plus. Such a set almost certainly requires one extra accessory, namely a VSWR meter, for ensuring that the antenna is correctly tuned to the frequency band of operation. The only other item required is the antenna itself. A typical base station antenna for 27 MHz consists of a base-loaded 1.5 metre long vertical rod mounted above four radials, known as a *ground-plane antenna*. The cost may vary somewhat but is in the region of £20 to £50 for one that is reasonably well made.

CB equipment for mobile operation is designed to run on the 12 V vehicle battery and the price of these sets is usually less than for a base station outfit. Prices range from around £40 to £90 or more depending on extra facilities that the manufacturer has chosen to incorporate. Such sets can of course be operated as a base station by using an external mains power supply for 240 V mains input with a 12 V dc regulated output. The antenna for 27 MHz must be base loaded only and nor more than 1.5 metres long. In this case no radials are necessary as the vehicle body, which must be of metal of course, will act as a ground plane. These antennas cannot be used on vehicles with fibreglass bodies nor can they be used on wing mirror arms on large commercial vehicles. The average price of a mobile antenna is about £10, with better quality types costing about £20 but as far as performance is concerned there is little difference.

Are callsigns for CB radio issued?

No callsigns are assigned either by the Home Office or the Post Office nor is an offical register of callsigns kept as is done for amateur radio. CB operators are free to identify themselves as they please, using their real names or one they have made up (called a 'handle'). See also Chapter 5.

Is there a good reason for using a callsign or handle?

There may be many reasons for not using your real name on the air. The major one is that you do not know who may be listening or for what reason. A CB conversation is not private like a telephone call, where (in normal circumstances) you can be reasonably sure that only the person called is listening. On CB anyone tuned to your channel can hear what you say, and it is possible that you may give information that will tell a house-breaker when your house will be unoccupied, or a thief when your car is unattended.

It is not unknown for a CB set to be stolen from the car while the owner is having a drink in a public house – because the owner told another CB user where he was and what he was doing.

Is it necessary to keep a log book?

There is no need under the CB licence to keep records of transmissions made and received. However, it is useful to keep a log book showing dates and times of transmissions, the callsigns of stations or persons contacted; details of radio and weather conditions prevailing at the time etc. if only from the point of view of personal interest. A log book is also useful in proving whether you were, or were not, on the air at some given time should a neighbour have cause to complain of television interference which you may, or may not, have caused.

Can a CB operator become a radio amateur?

Yes, but only after the Radio Amateur Examination has been taken and the appropriate pass certificate obtained, when a class

B amateur radio licence is issued, allowing operation on certain amateur bands. To obtain a Class A amateur radio licence it is necessary to pass in addition a morse code test of sending and receiving at 12 words per minute. The Class A licence enables a radio amateur to operate on all the amateur bands. For those interested, *Q and A on Amateur Radio* (Newnes Technical Books) is recommended. Further details about the amateur radio licence can be obtained from the Home Office Radio Regulatory Branch, Waterloo House, Waterloo Bridge Road, London SE1 8UA. Further information on the City and Guilds of London Institute Radio Amateurs' Examination can be obtained from City and Guilds of London Institute, 76 Portland Place, London W1N 4AA. Sample examination papers and statistical information are also available on request.

Can I set up my own CB station?

It is not difficult for anyone, even those with little technical knowledge, to set up a CB radio base station successfully, provided the instructions issued with the equipment are followed carefully. The trickiest part may be in setting up and tuning the transmitting antenna although with care it is not difficult. The installation of equipment for mobile operation also involves care and attention and there may be problems to overcome with interference caused by the car ignition system etc. Details of CB radio installations are given in a later chapter.

Can I use CB radio on holiday?

As already mentioned CB radio can be used in a car or boat and could of course be set up in a holiday bungalow or caravan, assuming permission is obtained if such premises are hired. Much the same applies to holiday boats on inland waterways. CB can otherwise be used on holiday anywhere in the UK but the licence issued by the Home Office does not permit the use of CB in countries outside the UK. The use or otherwise of CB on boats outside UK waters is not mentioned in the CB radio licence.

The frequency allocations, modulation and power levels etc., permitted in other countries may vary considerably so to use CB abroad you would need not only an appropriate licence, assuming that it would be issued in the first place by the country concerned, but the CB set would have to comply with whatever regulations applied in the country concerned.

As yet there are no agreements regarding the use of CB by UK citizens, even in the common market countries, although this facility is under consideration. Until some form of agreement is reached, which also involves bringing frequency allocations etc. into line, the best advice that can be given if you are going on holiday abroad, is to leave any CB equipment, mobile or portable, at home. In some countries even being in possession of a CB set is illegal and if discovered could put you in a serious and difficult situation. In other countries your set will be, or is likely to be, confiscated by Customs Authorities on entry and, if you are fortunate, returned to you when you leave.

What sources of information are there?

Apart from detailed technical books of both British and American origin there are at least a half dozen monthly magazines devoted to CB radio. Most books of American origin do not give accurate information on UK CB radio equipment and its operation, on frequency modulation or on the types of antennas that may only be used in the UK.

The UK CB Handbook, published by Newnes Technical Books, gives details of equipment and operation etc. There are numerous other British books on CB radio available.

Where can details of CB clubs and other organisations be obtained?

Names and addresses of local CB clubs are published regularly in most of the CB monthly magazines or can be obtained by writing to them. Further information about the CB radio REACT organisation is given in Chapter 5.

2
Technical matters

What are the differences between the two CB bands?

The 27 MHz band is the most popular, and whilst its use is the same as for the 934 MHz band, there are wide technical differences between the two. Efficient equipment for the 27 MHz band is produced at relatively low cost, and provides good results with simple omnidirectional antennas. One problem with 27 MHz however, can be the high degree of interference caused by continental CB stations operating single sideband (SSB) transmitters at high power levels and using very efficient directional antennas. These transmissions suffer virtually no attenuation since they arrive in this country by reflection from the ionosphere and can actually be much stronger than a transmission from a UK CB station only a mile or two away. The result is complete obliteration of the signal you are trying to receive. The antenna allowed for 27 MHz is not capable of transmitting a good signal over distances of 16 000 km (1000 miles) or more and the effective radiated power of 2 W, which is the maximum allowed, also severely limits the possibilities for long distance operation.

The 934 MHz band signals travel only over 'line of sight' distances, although there is often some extension of this range due to certain tropospheric (lower atmosphere) conditions that sometimes prevail. Equipment for 934 MHz is generally more expensive, including antennas which must be precisely designed in order to work efficiently. Because of the limited range of operation the 20 channels allowed can be used by several operators at

11

any one time provided the distance between them is more than the average line of sight range. Higher transmitting power is allowed for 934 MHz and a more efficient antenna may be used.

What is the Home Office Specification?

There are in fact two specifications: MPT1320 refers to 27 MHz equipment and MPT1321 to 934 MHz equipment. Each specification points out that all citizens' band radio equipment must be covered by a licence governing how the apparatus may be used and maintained to certain minimum required technical standards. The manufacturer, assembler, or importer of all citizens' band equipment is responsible for ensuring that the apparatus conforms with the specifications and any additional requirements imposed by regulations under the Wireless Telegraphy Act 1949. Conformity with the standards may be established by tests carried out by the manufacturer, assembler or importer or by a reputable test establishment, but in any case conformity with the specification remains the responsibility of the manufacturer, assembler or importer.

Note: These specifications and the requirements for performance also apply to anyone who makes or home assembles a CB set from components or from a kit of parts.

All purchasers and licensed owners of CB equipment should be acquainted with the contents of these specifications. Copies of the specifications MPT1320 and MPT1321 are available from the Stationery Office or any authorised Stationery Office agent.

What is the scope of the 27 MHz specification?

For the 27 MHz equipment the specification covers the minimum performance requirements for angle modulated equipment comprising base station, mobile or handheld transceivers or receivers only and any accessories, for example attenuators and vehicle adaptors, for optional use in the citizens' band service. For all equipment covered by this specification the nominal separation between adjacent channel carrier frequencies is 10 kHz.

What are the operating frequencies for 27 MHz?

The 40 radio frequency channels are shown in Table 1. CB radio equipment must not have facilities for transmission of radio frequencies other than those in Table 1, although 27 MHz equipment may be combined with 934 MHz equipment, when the channels shown in Table 2 may also be included. Only angle modulation is permitted.

Table 1. The frequencies and channel numbers allocated for the UK 27 MHz FM band

Channel	Frequency (MHz)	Channel	Frequency (MHz)
01	27.60125	21	27.80125
02	27.61125	22	27.81125
03	27.62125	23	27.82125
04	27.63125	24	27.83125
05	27.64125	25	27.84125
06	27.65125	26	27.85125
07	27.66125	27	27.86125
08	27.67125	28	27.87125
09	27.68125	29	27.88125
10	27.69125	30	27.89125
11	27.70125	31	27.90125
12	27.71125	32	27.91125
13	27.72125	33	27.92125
14	27.73125	34	27.93125
15	27.74125	35	27.94125
16	27.75125	36	27.95125
17	27.76125	37	27.96125
18	27.77125	38	27.97125
19	27.78125	39	27.98125
20	27.79125	40	27.99125

Tolerance ± 1.5 kHz

What are the operating frequencies for 934 MHz?

The 20 radio frequency channels are shown in Table 2. No other frequencies may be made available except for those in the 27 MHz band (Table 1), and only angle modulation is allowed.

Table 2. The frequencies and channel numbers allocated for the UK 934 MHz FM band

Channel	Frequency (MHz)	Channel	Frequency (MHz)
01	934.025	11	934.525
02	934.075	12	934.575
03	934.125	13	934.625
04	934.175	14	934.675
05	934.225	15	934.725
06	934.275	16	934.775
07	934.325	17	934.825
08	934.375	18	934.875
09	934.425	19	934.925
10	934.475	20	934.975

Tolerance ± 8.0 kHz

What is angle modulation?

This is a term covering *frequency modulation* and *phase modulation*, although the latter is not generally used in CB equipment, where only angle modulation is permitted.

What is modulation?

This is the name given to the modification applied to a radio frequency carrier produced by the transmitter in order to transmit speech, or other sound, or even morse code. The carrier wave is an alternating voltage which has constant amplitude and frequency; modulation can be achieved by (a) changing its amplitude as in Fig. 3, hence *amplitude modulation* (AM); (b) changing its frequency while keeping the amplitude constant, *frequency modulation* (FM); or (c) *phase modulation* (PM) where the carrier is

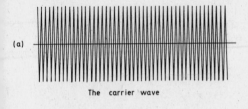

(a)

The carrier wave

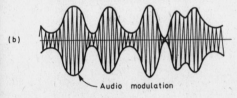

(b)

Audio modulation

Fig. 3. Amplitude modulation is produced by controlling the level of the carrier wave with audio signals. This system of modulation is not allowed in the UK for CB radio

rotated through part of a circle about its centre. At present this has no direct application in CB radio.

What is frequency modulation?

This form of modulation involves variation of the frequency of the master oscillator used to drive the transmitter. It can be achieved in several ways according to the nature of the master oscillator in use. In the case of a variable frequency oscillator (VFO) the frequency itself (see Fig. 4) can be varied by a reactance modulator which presents a varying reactance across the tuned

15

circuit of the VFO. Variations in the reactance caused by the audio modulating voltage will alter the VFO frequency. A change in oscillator frequency due to audio modulation can also be achieved by the use of a variable capacitance diode known as a varactor. When the fundamental oscillator frequency is multiplied, which it normally is to reach the final frequency of

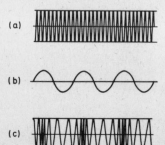

Fig. 4. Frequency modulation: (a) the normal carrier wave; (b) the audio signal: (c) the carrier frequency is changed according to the level of the audio signal applied

transmission, the frequency deviation produced by modulation is multiplied by the same factor. Thus the deviation of the oscillator frequency must be adjusted to take into account the frequency multiplication used to reach the final transmitting frequency. The final frequency deviation is usually in the region of 2.5 to 5 kHz.

What is single sideband (SSB) modulation?

Fig. 3 shows a double sideband AM waveform. One sideband is shown as the part above the centre line, the other sideband is below the centre line.

A single sideband (SSB) transmitter has to perform two distinct functions. One is the suppression of the carrier wave and the other the complete elimination of one sideband. The carrier is suppressed by feeding the output of the carrier frequency oscillator and modulating voltage into a balanced modulator, a form of bridge circuit which, correctly balanced, will suppress the carrier input so that only two sidebands appear at the output. The unwanted sideband is then removed by a filter. An SSB transmitter is an extremely complex piece of equipment and further discussion is beyond the scope of this book. It is important to remember that single sideband operation for CB radio is not allowed in the UK although its use by many continental CB operators can and does cause serious interference with the UK FM CB system. Amplitude modulation is not permitted in the UK for CB radio although it is used by CB operators in other countries. There are however, many CB operators in the UK using amplitude and SSB modulation illegally on the American CB channels which are between 26.965 and 27.950 MHz. Many AM sets of American origin do not conform to the UK specifications and can cause interference from sideband splatter.

What is sideband splatter?

Any form of AM signal of high intensity and particularly one on which the modulation is above a normal working level, i.e. above 100%, or where excessive sideband is being generated in the case of SSB, can cause spurious signals to be generated which will produce the effect of broken distorted speech, sometimes in the form of random noise that spreads over several channels either side of the frequency on which the transmission is being made. This effect is very noticeable if the selectivity of the receiver is poor, i.e. the tuning is not sharp enough to reject interfering signals from adjacent channels.

What is deviation?

A representation of frequency modulation is shown in Fig. 4. When a modulating signal is applied the carrier frequency is increased during one half cycle of the modulating signal and decreased during the half cycle of opposite polarity. This is indicated in the diagram by the RF cycles occupying less time (higher frequency) when the modulating signal is positive and

17

more time (lower frequency) when the modulating signal is negative. The change in the carrier frequency, called frequency deviation, is proportional to the instantaneous amplitude of the modulating signal. Therefore the deviation is small when the instantaneous amplitude of the modulating signal is small and greatest when the modulating signal reaches its peak, either positive or negative. The amplitude of the signal, i.e. the RF carrier, does not change during modulation.

What is the capture effect?

When a signal is being received on FM it can be completely over-ridden by a stronger signal on the same frequency, i.e. the stronger signal 'captures' the frequency.

What is an 'S' meter?

These meters are normally included in all receivers and transceivers intended for communication purposes and usually have a calibration similar to that shown at the top of Fig 5. As the initial letter 'S' indicates, the meter is for reading the signal strength of

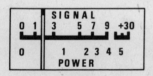

Fig. 5. Typical signal level and power indication meter found on most CB sets. The top scale indicates the strength of incoming signals from S0 to S9 and up to +30 dB. The bottom scale indicates the power output in watts when the set is switched to transmit

the transmission being received. The calibration of such meters usually runs from 0 to 9, the figures being used to express the level as S1, S2, S3 etc. Above S9 meters are often calibrated in decibels, the figures indicating the level of the signal when it is greater than the highest value of S9, i.e. the signal strength can be said to be so many dBs above S9. Calibration of meters varies considerably and should not be accepted as standard. The scale at the bottom of Fig. 5 indicates the transmitter power output.

What is meant by transmitter power output?

This is the power delivered to the antenna terminal by the final amplifier in the transmitter. The small amount of power generated by the master oscillator, which in case of FM transmission may also be modulated, is amplified by a number of stages until the requisite output power from the transmitter is achieved. For CB 27 MHz FM transceivers the maximum power output allowed by the UK CB licence is 4 W and for 934 MHz FM CB radio is 8 W. If the transceiver is functioning according to the manufacturer's specification then the power levels mentioned above should be exactly as measured with an accurate power meter coupled to a dummy load of 50 ohms. The output impedance of CB transceivers is standardised on 50 ohms.

What is meant by effective radiated power?

Effective radiated power (ERP) is normally that which is actually transmitted by the antenna and is not necessarily the same as the output power from the transceiver. For example if the use of a natural dipole antenna were allowed for CB radio then assuming no feed cable loss the power radiated from the dipole would be in the region of 90% of the output power from the transmitter, when it could be said that the effective radiated power would be 90% of 4 W or 3.6W. However, under the terms of the CB licence for 27 MHz the ERP must not exceed 2 W, which is 50% of the power fed to the antenna. In order to achieve this the antenna itself would need to be at least a full quarter-wavelength ground-plane or similar antenna with an efficiency of about 50%. But the antenna permitted by the licence must have a physical length of not more than 1.5 metres and because of this the efficiency is limited to only 3 or 4% which means that of the 4 W output from the transmitter only 0.16 W is actually radiated. This applies to both base and mobile operation for which the specified type of antenna must be used.

On 934 MHz the situation is much better since an ERP of up to 25 W is permissible. This means that the ERP may be 3.125 times the 8 W power output from the transmitter and which is 25 W. Therefore an antenna which has some power gain may be used. The gain required to achieve an ERP of 25 W is approximately 5 dB. Any antenna used for 934 MHz may have this amount of gain which incidentally is relative to a single fully resonant half-wave dipole. (Antennas are dealt with in greater detail in Chapter 4.)

How do the CB channel numbers relate to the listed frequencies?

The channel numbers and their related frequencies for the UK CB radio FM band are given in Table 1. The nominal separation between adjacent carrier frequencies is therefore 10 kHz. The channel numbers and related frequencies for 934 MHz are given in Table 2. The separation between adjacent channels will be seen as 50 kHz. The frequency tolerance for each channel for the 27 MHz band is ± 1.5 kHz and for the 934 MHz band the frequency tolerance per channel is ± 8 kHz.

What are the common controls on a CB transceiver?

Fig. 6 shows a typical 27 MHz CB radio transceiver and the positions and names of the various controls. The main *channel control* switches the transmitter to any one of the 40 available channels, the number of which appears as an LED readout. The *squelch control* is used to mute the high level background noise which is due to the high gain of the receiving amplifier stages so that the set itself is effectively silent until a signal is received on the channel. The *volume control* adjusts the loudness of the signal being received. Some sets have what is called a *local/DX* switch which is simply a switched attenuator to assist in reducing the level of very strong incoming signals. All approved CB sets must carry a switch either on the front panel, or at the rear, to

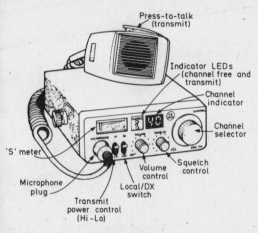

Fig. 6. Typical 27 MHz approved CB radio transmitter showing the various controls. Some sets have additional refinements as mentioned in the text

attenuate the transmitter power output from 4 W down to 0.4 W, i.e. by 10 dB, when the antenna used with the set is at a height above ground exceeding 7 metres. Most sets have an '*S' meter*, although this may be a dual purpose type that also enables readings of VSWR (voltage standing wave ratio) to be obtained when tuning the antenna for resonance and matching. Most sets are supplied with a hand-held type microphone with a PTT (press-to-talk) switch, and some have a PA facility.

21

How is a transceiver switched from receive to transmit?

The push-to-talk switch on the microphone operates a relay which (a) connects the microphone to the transmitter input; (b) switches the antenna from receiver input to transmitter output; (c) disconnects the loudspeaker. Fig. 7 shows the basic functions.

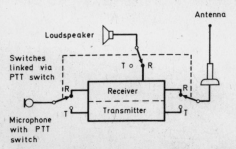

Fig. 7. *Basic receiver/transmitter switching showing how microphone, antenna and loudspeaker connections are switched from receive to transmit*

How does a CB radio work?

The basic block diagram of Fig. 8 shows the main parts comprising a transceiver and how they are interconnected. Some sets use a crystal controlled oscillator to generate a 9 MHz carrier which is then modulated and multiplied by three to produce the 27 MHz modulated radio frequency. Other sets use a phase locked loop synthesiser (PLL) to produce the RF.

What is a PA facility?

Some CB sets have a switch marked PA or PA facility which enables the microphone to be switched directly through to the receiver output amplifier enabling microphone talk-through to

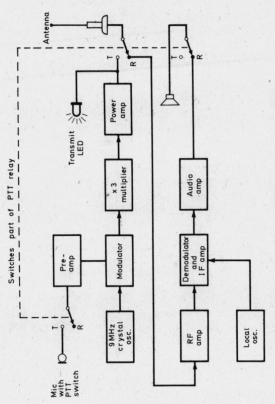

Fig. 8. Block diagram of a set using a crystal-controlled oscillator

Antenna

Switches part of PTT relay

Transmit LED

Power amp

× 3 multiplier

Pre-amp

Modulator

9 MHz crystal osc.

Mic with PTT switch

Audio amp

Demodulator and IF amp

RF amp

Local osc.

23

the loudspeaker, i.e. so that the set can be used as a form of loud hailer or public address system. Such a facility has little or no real use, so it is not important that the set you purchase has this incorporated.

What is speech processing?

Some of the more expensive CB transceivers may have built-in provision for what is called speech processing. The object is to maintain a constant level of speech signals from the microphone, i.e. to account for quiet speaking or very loud speaking in such a way that all the speech is transmitted at an even level and therefore modulation (or deviation) is also maintained at a maximum level. These systems help to improve readability, particularly when received signals are weak and affected by noise and interference. If the deviation level and microphone gain in a CB transceiver are properly adjusted there is little or no need for the use of speech processors for FM transmission. Such a facility is only really effective on SSB transmission.

Can a mobile set be operated from a separate power supply?

All CB radio transceivers intended for mobile use operate from what is normally regarded as a 12 V supply, i.e. a car battery, although they are designed to work at a maximum rail voltage of 13.8 V. These sets can be removed from the vehicle and used for base station operation by running them directly from an external 12 V car battery but this is a rather dangerous practice in enclosed spaces because of the fumes given off by the battery. The best method of running a mobile CB transceiver is to use an external power supply which draws power from the normal house mains supply and provides a fully regulated 13.8 V d.c. supply for the transceiver. It is very important that a power supply capable of delivering the full current required by the transceiver is used. In most cases a power supply of 13.8 V with a current capacity of about 5 A will suffice. *Warning:* Cheap power supplies are often very poorly regulated and will not always supply the rated current; consequently they may have an output voltage well below 13.8 V when running on load.

Can AM and SSB transceivers be converted for FM use?

It is possible that some sets can be converted provided they are reasonably up to date and have modern integrated circuitry and other components. Older type sets from the USA may not lend themselves to this modification. However, the job must be carried out by a competent engineer with appropriate test equipment in order that compliance with the specifications are met when modifications have been completed. Anyone owning such a set can therefore only really consult the manufacturer, a competent CB dealer, or anyone specialising in carrying out such modifications.

What is a handheld set?

These are small complete transmitter/receivers for hand use and are sometimes known as walkie-talkies. They are completely self-contained and generally operate from internal dry batteries or rechargeable batteries. Some of those available comply with the Home Office specifications and are intended for normal operation on the UK CB FM band. However, there are many sets designed to operate only on 49 MHz and/or some other frequency and these are *not* legal in the UK. Operation of any transmitter on unauthorised frequencies can cause serious interference to other and often vital communications services.

Are direct telephone links with CB radio legal?

Telephone systems may not be connected to CB transmitter/ receivers for remote use or indeed to any other radio system unless they have been approved by British Telecom. There are also a number of telephone radio link systems advertised but which are not approved by British Telecom since they operate on unallocated frequencies.

Can CB radio be used on boats at sea?

Since the CB licence allows the use of sets on *any* vehicle except aircraft, CB transceivers may be legally used on boats operating at sea. However, there is no facility for contact directly with Coastguard or other coastal communication services. It would be unwise to rely entirely on CB radio for emergency calls in cases of distress as there is no fully established monitoring service. The chances of being heard by stations on shore could be very remote particularly when radio conditions are poor and also in view of the range limitations imposed by the type of antenna and output power allowed for CB radio.

What is a scanner receiver?

This is a system where the receiver automatically tunes itself over pre-selected channels or all the channels available, one after the other. When a signal is sensed on a particular channel the receiver stops scanning and locks onto the signal so that it can be heard. Usually when the signal ceases the scanning system resumes its function and continues until another signal appears on one of the frequencies.

Can Police calls be heard with a CB transceiver?

Police calls cannot be received on a properly adjusted transceiver and furthermore convertors or other add-on units must not be used with CB equipment that will enable Police, Fire, Ambulance or other transmissions to be received.

What criteria should be used when buying a CB transceiver?

Whilst an expert is able to read and understand the specifications that apply to radio and other electronic equipment and can draw his own conclusions, anyone without specific knowledge will mostly have to depend on the integrity of the CB equipment dealer. The fact that a brand name may not be well known is not necessarily an indication that the product is inferior. On the other hand one can be equally suspicious of equipment carrying well known brand names. Magazines devoted to CB radio publish test reports on equipment but one should be assured that performance tests have been properly carried out by experts with the necessary laboratory equipment to back up their findings (see also Chapter 3).

What is meant by E.I.A. standard?

This simply means that electronic and radio equipment, including CB radio sets, have been designed to conform with the technical standards and requirements of the Electronic Industries Association. This generally applies to equipment manufactured in the USA.

Does the number of transistors incorporated in a CB transceiver give any indication of its capability?

The answer to this is either no, or not necessarily. For example, if a transceiver employs integrated circuits any one particular integrated circuit might contain a half dozen or more transistors which could not be included in a total count of the transistors used in the set. Modern transceivers in fact tend to use more integrated circuits than individual transistors.

What is meant by receiver sensitivity?

This is the measure of the receptivity of the receiver or receiving section of a transceiver. For example if the sensitivity is given as 1 μV (microvolt) for 10 dB S/N (signal to noise), it means that a radio signal only one millionth of one volt in strength at the antenna terminal will produce a sound in the loudspeaker which will contain speech signal power of ten times the noise power. A receiver rated at 0.5 μV for 20 dB S/N would be considered quite sensitive whereas a rating of 2 μV for say 10 dB S/N would be very poor.

What is meant by receiver selectivity?

Selectivity means the ability to reject signals on channels other than the channel to which the transceiver is set. A transceiver which has poor selectivity will allow the reception of signals from channels adjacent to the one actually being used. The effect of poor selectivity would be most noticeable where several CB stations were operating very close to each other.

What is a linear amplifier?

This is an amplifier with an output that rises linearly as the input signal is increased. Such amplifiers are used to boost the output from a small transmitter, for example an output of say 4 W or more while still retaining the original modulation. This type of amplifier is not legal in the UK and although used illegally are frequently the cause of high level interference to other sevices, especially television.

What is harmonic radiation?

All transmitters are capable of generating harmonics related to the fundamental frequency, e.g. second, third, fourth and so on, and if these are unsuppressed can cause inteference to radio services using frequencies the same as those of the harmonics. For example, the fourth harmonic from a 27 MHz CB transmitter can cause interference to aircraft radio instrument landing systems. On well-designed sets such harmonics are suppressed to the greatest possible extent often to as much as 60 dB or more, i.e. 1 millionth of the level of the fundamental transmission. When harmonics are found to be the cause of interference then suppression can often be effected by using special filters connected in the output from the transmitter.

What are spurious transmissions?

Harmonics from a transmitter are sometimes referred to as 'spurious signals', but there are cases where signals not directly related to the fundamental can be generated within a transmitter because of instability in the circuitry. Spurious signals can often occur at frequencies totally unrelated to either the fundamental or any harmonics due to the fundamental, but nevertheless can cause interference to other services, e.g. TVI and BCI.

What is TVI and BCI?

The terms stand for television interference (TVI) and broadcast interference (BCI) and mean that such services are being interfered with by transmissions usually on frequencies not directly related to those of the television or broadcast transmissions. Interfering signals are frequently due to harmonics or spurious radiation from a transmitter or can be due to direct breakthrough of the fundamental transmission. Television receivers, broadcast receivers and modern hi-fi systems are very prone to interference caused by direct breakthrough of a signal from a transmitter operating on frequencies quite remote from the frequencies used for television or broadcasting.

29

What is a filter?

These are devices used for either acceptance of wanted frequencies or rejection of unwanted frequencies. Special filters which reject all frequencies above the fundamental or wanted frequency are known as *low pass filters*, while filters which reject low frequencies and pass only high frequencies are known as *high pass filters*.

What is cross modulation?

This occurs in reception and may take place if a strong unwanted signal is overloading the receiver input circuits. The unwanted station will then be heard as a background to the wanted signal.

What is a dummy load?

This is a purely resistive device which may be substituted for a normal antenna, i.e. to represent the load otherwise imposed by the antenna and thereby used to absorb the output power from a transmitter. A dummy load is normally only used for test purposes and its resistance must always equal the output impedance of the transmitter. For example if the transmitter output impedance is 50 ohms then a dummy load connected to the transmitter must have a pure self-resistance of 50 ohms.

What are decibels?

Most people associate decibels with sound level. The decibel system is, however, used to express relative levels of other electrical units for virtually no other reason than being a more convenient way of doing so. The decibel is not a measure of any particular electrical unit and figures given as decibels have no meaning unless related to a given reference. A decibel, which is one tenth of a *bel*, is derived from the logarithmic ratio of two

Table 3. Decibels (dB) represent the ratio of one power to another, or one voltage to another at the same impedance. Decibels are either *positive* for a gain, or *negative* for a loss.

Voltage loss	Power loss	dB	Voltage gain	Power gain
1.000	1.000	0	1.000	1.000
0.981	0.977	0.1	1.012	1.023
0.977	0.955	0.2	1.023	1.047
0.966	0.933	0.3	1.035	1.072
0.955	0.912	0.4	1.047	1.096
0.944	0.891	0.5	1.059	1.122
0.933	0.871	0.6	1.072	1.148
0.912	0.832	0.8	1.096	1.202
0.891	0.794	1.0	1.122	1.259
0.794	0.631	2.0	1.259	1.585
0.708	0.501	3.0	1.413	.1995
0.631	0.398	4.0	1.585	2.512
0.562	0.316	5.0	1.778	3.162
0.501	0.251	6.0	1.995	3.981
0.447	0.200	7.0	2.239	5.012
0.398	0.159	8.0	2.512	6.310
0.355	0.126	9.0	2.818	7.943
0.316	0.100	10.0	3.162	10.0
0.200	0.0398	14.0	5.01	25.1
0.100	0.0100	20.0	10.00	100.00
3.16×10^{-2}	10^{-3}	30.0	3.16×10	10^3
10^{-2}	10^{-4}	40.0	10^2	10^4
3.16×10^{-3}	10^{-5}	50.0	3.16×10^2	10^5
10^{-3}	10^{-6}	60.0	10^3	10^6
3.16×10^{-4}	10^{-7}	70.0	3.16×10^3	10^7
10^{-4}	10^{-8}	80.0	10^4	10^8
3.16×10^{-5}	10^{-9}	90.0	3.16×10^4	10^9
10^{-5}	10^{-10}	100.0	10^5	10^{10}

dBs can be added to represent a total gain or loss, while the gain or losses expressed as fractions of decibels must be multiples, e.g. A power gain of 3.5 dB is 3.0 dB plus 0.5 dB, which is

$$1.995 \ (3.0 \, dB) \times 1.122 \ (0.5 \, dB) = 2.384.$$

voltages or current or power levels. One of these levels, which can of course be measured, must be given as a reference otherwise the figure quoted in decibels (dB) is meaningless. Table 3 shows decibels as related to voltage and power ratios. The ratios applied to voltage are the same as for current measurements.

Is there any danger from radiation at 934 MHz?

It has been said that radiation at frequencies in the region of 900 to 1000 MHz (and higher) can have undesirable effects on human tissue. This has not been fully proved although there have been claimed cases of eye damage thought to be due to exposure to radiation in this frequency range. It is a known fact that the concentration of power per square centimetre is high, much higher than obtained at lower frequencies, such as 27 MHz. It is possible of course that some people might be affected, but this could only be caused by very close proximity to an antenna radiating relatively high power. Close proximity means within a few inches of an antenna so the only advice that can be given is − don't stand with your head very close to an antenna to which power is being applied at 934 MHz.

Can I build my own CB rig?

Kits of parts for the home construction of CB equipment are available and those with the requisite technical knowledge and test equipment will no doubt be able to build CB equipment from published circuits. However, any home constructed equipment must comply in every sense with the performance specifications set down by the Home Office in the publications MPT1320 (27 MHz) and MPT1321 (934 MHz).

What is VOX?

VOX means 'voice operated switch' and enables voice actuation of a transmitter thus eliminating the need to use the transmitter button on the microphone or on the set. In other words directly the operator speaks the VOX system automatically switches the transmitter on and it will remain so until the operator stops speaking.

What is meant by selective calling?

Selective calling (Selcal) is allowed by the terms of the UK CB licence and means that a CB transceiver may be equipped with a selective calling encoder which transmits different tones or combinations of tones to signal other transceivers individually. The receiving transceivers are equipped with decoders which cause the loudspeaker to be muted until a specific tone or combination of tones is intercepted. Thus no signals are audible until the tone signalling system is operated.

3
Equipment for CB radio

What is the minimum equipment needed for mobile operation?

A good deal of CB radio operation is mobile and the basic requirements are an approved transceiver operating directly from the 12 V vehicle battery. The sets are normally supplied with a microphone and the only other essential item is a suitable mobile antenna. The only accessory likely to be required will be a VSWR meter for tuning the antenna, unless the set itself has built-in meter for this purpose. Even the low cost sets have all the essential controls plus a digital readout channel indicator and a signal level meter and are in the price range £40 to £80. For the inclusion of refinements such as a built-in VSWR meter and combined power output meter, automatic channel scanning, and delta control (fine tuning control) etc. one will have to pay a little more, probably between £90 and £100. Apart from a VSWR meter there are few other accessories that could be considered as essential.

What is the minimum equipment for home (base) station operation?

Transceivers for home operation are mains powered for a nominal 230 V mains supply but otherwise have the same electrical performance as mobile transceivers. The facilities are also similar for example, the set will have a channel selection control, channel number digital readout, a signal level meter, squelch control, volume control and power reduction switch, and are also supplied with a handheld microphone. The only other essential item is of course a base station antenna and the only accessory needed is a VSWR meter. Sets in the higher price bracket normally include a combined strength, VSWR and antenna power meter, a fine tuning control and automatic monitoring of one or two selected channels, for instance the emergency channel 9. All CB transceivers, base station or mobile, should have built-in protection against transistor power output stage breakdown which could occur in the event of open or short circuit connections at the antenna output, or at the antenna itself, or because of very high VSWR. The price range for low cost sets is in the region of £60 to £80 and for those with added refinements £80 to £100 plus.

Is it difficult to install a mobile CB transceiver?

With a little care and a few precautions there are not many difficulties likely to arise in installing a CB transceiver in a car. The normal location for a CB set is under the dashboard as shown in Fig. 9, although some thought should be given to ease of use

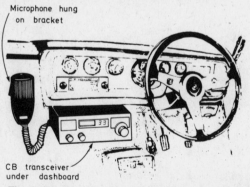

Microphone hung on bracket

CB transceiver under dashboard

Fig. 9. *Most mobile sets are installed under the dashboard although there are sets available that can be remote controlled from the microphone and therefore housed out of sight in the boot or under a seat*

whilst driving. For example it might be preferable to have the microphone available for operation in the right hand to avoid the possibility of the microphone cord becoming entangled with the gear lever etc. It is important that the 12 V supply leads be taken direct from the battery terminals but the positive lead must include an in-line fuse. Most sets are built for negative earth operation so make sure that your vehicle has a negative earth battery. *Note:* Some CB sets will operate from either a positive or negative earthed supply.

Are mounting facilities provided for mobile sets?

Almost all mobile transceivers are supplied complete with a mounting frame with the necessary screws and fittings as shown in Fig. 10. Most frames have a quick release system so that the set

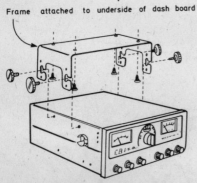

Frame attached to underside of dash board

Fig. 10. *Mobile transceivers are equipped with a holding frame for attachment under the dashboard, many of which have a quick release facility for removal of the set*

can be withdrawn easily if if it is required for use elsewhere or to prevent theft when the car is left parked. There are some mobile sets where the main transmitter/receiver section can be mounted in the boot or some other convenient place and remote controlled from the driving position by means of a special handheld combined microphone and control panel.

Can equipment intended for mobile operated be used on boats?

Any type of mobile CB equipment intended for operation from a 12 V battery can be used on a boat provided of course that a battery is available. There may be problems with antennas since the specified base loaded antenna for 27 MHz will not function on fibreglass or wooden boats unless a ground-plane is provided. The only other real precautions to be taken are protection of the equipment against salt water and damp. Ideally any radio equipment should be located in a position where damp and moisture cannot get in, not easy to find on most small boats.

Is there a wide range of sets from which to choose?

There are certainly plenty of CB transceivers of different makes to choose from although most are of Japanese or other Far Eastern manufacture. You would be wise to study the manufacturers' specifications, read as many reviews as possible, and consult with your CB dealer before purchasing. Many 27 MHz transceivers have been found widely adrift on performance as laid down in MPT1320, despite carrying the Home Office approval label (CB27/81) for 27 MHz equipment. On many sets the following performance factors have been found somewhat poor. *Sensitivity:* Some with worse than 1 μV for 10 dB S/N, which is not particularly good. *Selectivity:* On some sets this is so poor that separation of strong signals on adjacent channels is virtually impossible, e.g. a local transmission could capture two or three other channels simultaneously. *Frequency stability:* Individual channels not properly tuned to the channel frequency and therefore impossible to use. *Harmonics and other spurious radiation:* Some sets produce harmonics strong enough to cause serious interference to services on very high frequencies and also capable of producing severe television interference. *Power output:* Some sets do not produce the specified 4 W from a nominal regulated 13.8 V supply. *Power attenuation:* The switch provided should reduce the nominal power output of 4 W (by 10 dB) to 0.4 W. On some sets this was found to be as low as 0.1 W due to the attenuation control producing a drop in power by 16 dB instead of the specified 10 dB.

What is a typical performance specification for a CB transceiver?

The manufacturer's specification should be very carefully studied before purchase and readers are advised to read test reports or reviews of equipment published in the popular CB magazines. A typical specification for both transmitter and receiver sections of a CB set is shown in Table 4.

What are the performance requirements for CB radio equipment?

For 27 MHz the parameters from MPT1320 are as follows:

Frequencies: 27.60125–27.99125 MHz, in 40 channels 10 kHz apart
Frequency tolerance: ±1.5 kHz
Maximum power output from transmitter: 4 W
Maximum effective radiated power: 2 W
Modulation: Frequency or phase modulation
Deviation: ±2.5 kHz maximum
Power in adjacent channels: 60 dB down at 10 kHz or further away from carrier
Spurious radiation (transmitter): Below 50 nW between 80 and 85 MHz, 87.5–118 MHz, 135–136 MHz, 174–230 MHz and 470–862 MHz
Below 250 nW at any other frequency
(receiver): Below 20 nW at any frequency

Table 4. Typical specification for a CB transceiver

General

Channels	40 channels PLL digital logic synthesiser circuitry
Power requirement	Consumption 18 W. Current drain 1.3 A (100% mod) at 13.8 V dc
Power supply	12 V dc nominal positive or negative ground
Semiconductors	Integrated circuits, transistors and diodes
Operating temperature range	−30 to +50°C
Microphone	Dynamic with push to talk switch. 500 ohms
Built-in speaker	Impedance 8 ohms 3 inches diameter
Controls	Volume with on/off switch, squelch control, channel selector, CB/PA control, RF gain control, Delta tune etc
Connectors	External speaker 3.5 mm jack, Antenna connector, SO259 for coaxial plug 50 ohms. 12 V power jack
Circuit protection	System prevents transistor burn out when transmitting without antenna (5 minute limit). 2 A fuse in dc power cord

---

Receiver

Sensitivity	Better than 0.5 μV for 500 mW audio output at minimum position of squelch setting
Frequency range	27.60125 to 27.99125 MHz (40 channels)
Audio output power	At 10% distortion better than 2.2 W
Squelch range	0.5 μV nominal for 20 dB S/N

Transmitter

Frequency range	As above for receiving. 40 channels
Transmit power output	4 W maximum
Modulation	Capable of 3 kHz (full deviation) factory pre-set 2.5 kHz
Power output attenuation	By 10 dB

For 934 MHz the parameters from MPT1321 are as follows:

Frequencies: 934.025–934.975 MHz, in 20 channels 50 kHz apart

Frequency tolerance: ±8 kHz

Maximum power output from transmitter: 8 W

Maximum effective radiated power: 25 W

Modulation: Frequency or phase modulation

Deviation: ±5 kHz maximum

Power in adjacent channels: 60 dB down at 50 kHz or further away from carrier

Spurious radiation (transmitter): Below 50 nW between 70 and 230 MHz, 450–862 MHz. Below 240 nW at any other frequency.

(receiver): Below 20 nW at any frequency

Maximum effective radiated power (ERP) means the power that may actually be radiated by the antenna. For 27 MHz this is limited to 2 W or less by virtue of the specified antenna. For 934 MHz an antenna that has a gain of about 5 dB is permitted which will raise the ERP to 25 W.

Are conversion units for 27 MHz to 934 MHz operation available?

Converter units that will transform the output from a 27 MHz transmitter to 934 MHz are available and function on the basis that they will also receive 934 MHz signals and convert them to 27 MHz for listening in the normal way.

Can home built equipment be used?

While the answer is yes, it would be inadvisable to try building CB equipment from published circuits unless you have the technical knowledge and experience and also appropriate testing equipment available to prove that when finished, the set is capable of performing to Home Office specifications. Much the same applies to kits that are available because without test gear there is no way of proving that the finished product is functioning as it should and according to the Home Office specifications.

What equipment is considered illegal?

All CB sets that operate on the American CB frequencies and are equipped only for amplitude or sideband modulation are illegal. The frequency range of these sets is from 26.965 MHz to 27.405 MHz although they bear the same channel numbers as those for legal operation in the UK. There are many of these sets about and many will be offered for sale secondhand. It is up to the purchaser to make absolutely sure that he is not buying a set that would be considered illegal, the use of which could involve severe penalties. Other CB equipment that is illegal are frequency expander units which alter the set frequencies of a regular channelised CB set and linear amplifiers capable of delivering a power in excess of 4 W. Most linear amplifiers are rated for power levels of up to 100 W or more and use of these is very definitely illegal. All antennas except the 1.5 m base-loaded type are also illegal. Much the same applies to equipment for 934 MHz, i.e. linear amplifiers and antennas that do not meet the Home Office specification are classified as illegal.

Are modifications to CB equipment allowed?

Modifications may be made to CB equipment provided that the performance of the equipment still conforms with MPT1320 and MPT1321.

Are speech processors allowed?

The function of a speech processor was explained in the previous chapter and its use is not illegal. For FM operation the use of a speech processor has little effect, particularly if the deviation and microphone gain controls on the CB set are properly adjusted in the first place.

Is it advisable to attempt repairs to CB equipment?

Unless one has the necessary technical knowledge and testing equipment and also the circuit and other information concerned with the set, it would be most unwise to attempt any but very simple repairs, such as replacing a broken fuse or a disconnected external wire, etc. It is advisable take the set to a competent dealer or service engineer.

What other type of CB equipment is available?

The only other type of complete CB transceiver is the handheld set, more popularly known as a walkie-talkie. A typical model is shown in Fig. 11. These sets are powered by internal batteries and have a small telescopic antenna. Some have a built-in microphone whilst others use an external microphone. The facilities provided are similar to those found on regular CB sets although sometimes only a limited number of channels are provided. *Warning:* There are many handheld or walkie-talkie types sets available that operate on 49 MHz and 29 MHz which are not allocated frequencies. The use of such sets is illegal.

How should a home base CB system be set up?

Fig. 12 gives a rough idea of how a CB set and its associated accessories could be set up to provide (a) ease of convenience or operating and (b) keeping all the equipment together tidily in one place. Ideally radio equipment of this nature should be kept out of reach of very young children who could, if the set is connected to its supply, easily switch on and cause interference to others by

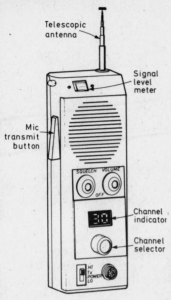

Telescopic antenna

Signal level meter

Mic transmit button

Channel indicator

Channel selector

Fig. 11. *A typical handheld (walkie-talkie) portable CB transceiver. The facilities are similar to those on conventional sets except that the antenna is built in and is telescopic. The range of these sets is limited to only a mile or so*

playing around with the controls especially with the set transmitting. When the set is not in use the safest way of preventing use and also as a precaution against electric shock etc., is to disconnect it from the mains supply.

What must be done if a CB set is causing interference to other services?

First some tests should be carried out to make sure that it is your set that is causing interference. If this is verified then it is obvious that the set should not be used until the cause of the interference is ascertained. Interference can be caused by excessive harmonic content from the transmitter, in which it may be necessary to fit a low pass filter between the set and the antenna lead. Typical

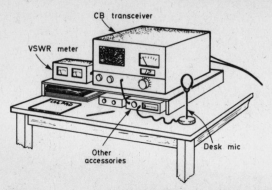

Fig. 12. A convenient arrangement for a base or home station for keeping equipment tidy and providing a comfortable operating position with everything to hand

filters are shown in Fig. 13. Interference can be caused by breakthrough of a transmitted carrier into the circuitry of television sets and hi-fi equipment, in which case the cause is not necessarily due to the transmitter, but in fact to the poor design of the television or hi-fi equipment. Carrier breakthrough often occurs when a TV or hi-fi system has a complete lack of screening around its own circuitry. There are numerous methods other than the use of filters for stopping interference but in case of real

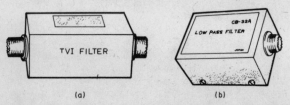

Fig. 13. Two typical harmonic filters for prevention of interference to other services operating at higher frequencies. (a) A filter specially designed for eliminating television interference, (b) a low-pass filter which does more or less the same job. Either may be fitted between the CB transceiver antenna socket and the feed cable to the antenna

44

difficulty it is advisable to consult the British Telecom Radio Interference Department. Application forms for interference investigations can be obtained at most Post Offices.

Can an indoor antenna be used?

Yes, and there are two possibilities here: one is to have the CB equipment in the living room and its antenna in a loft space, or even in an upstairs room, in order to gain a little height. Another

Fig. 14. Floor-stand antennas are available, although antennas for CB radio can be fitted into a loft space. As will all antennas used indoors the working range will be somewhat restricted

is a floor stand antenna so that the set and the antenna can be operated together in the same room. Such an arrangement may be found useful for residents in blocks of flats where external antennas cannot be used. A typical system is shown in Fig. 14.

Are sets available for use on the 934 MHz band?

At the time of writing there is one set available for operation on 934 MHz and more are in process of development. Owing to the sophisticated nature of the electronics involved and the special

45

circuitry for the very high frequency at which these sets operate, they are more expensive than sets designed for operation on 27 MHz. Antennas and other special accessories for this frequency band are also more expensive.

Are the various accessories including antennas readily available?

A wide range of useful accessories and different types of antenna are available from both large and small CB dealers. Many are of American, Japanese or other Far East origin and you should make sure that what you purchase is a quality product and will perform to the specification given by the manufacturer.

What is a VSWR meter?

Popularly known as a SWR-meter, this is one of the most important CB accessories and whilst some of the more expensive transceivers have them built in, it is necessary with most models to purchase one separately. The use of a VSWR meter is the only way to accurately tune the transmitting antenna to resonance, i.e.

Fig. 15. A typical dual meter VSWR bridge. The centre control is set to indicate the power output from the radio. When this is done the meter on the right will indicate the VSWR or voltage standing wave ratio

to the frequency of operation and to ensure at the same time that the antenna is correctly matched to the output of the transmitter. Low cost VSWR meters are not capable of reading VSWR at 934 MHz. Some VSWR meters have only a single scale for reading power after which the instrument is switched to read the actual VSWR (voltage standing wave ratio) (Fig. 15). A very

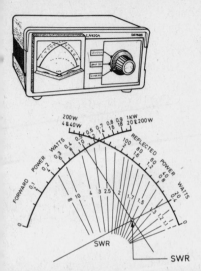

Fig. 16. (a) A dual-reading single-scale SWR meter with a high degree of accuracy. It has a working range of 20 to 1000 W. Direct power and VSWR readings are obtained instantly on the dual scale as shown in (b). The right-hand pointer is reading power on the top left-hand scale whilst the left-hand pointer is reading SWR on the lower right-hand scale

accurate but more expensive dual reading meter is shown in Fig. 16a. This has a twin scale and is in fact two meters combined in one. The power output is read on one scale and the SWR is read by a separate pointer on another scale as shown in Fig. 16b.

What is VSWR?

The VSWR (often called simply SWR) is the ratio of the signal voltage passing down a transmission line to the antenna compared with the reflected wave from the antenna. If the transmission line is the correct length and impedance and if the antenna is correctly tuned to the frequency being transmitted (i.e. if it is the

47

correct length) then all the signal from the transmitter will be radiated by the antenna. However, if the antenna or the transmission line (the cable) are not exactly correct, a small portion of the voltage wave arriving at the antenna will be reflected, rather like ripples on water when they reach an obstruction, to form 'standing waves' in the antenna system. The ratio of forward voltage to reflected voltage is the 'voltage standing wave ratio', VSWR. Generally a VSWR of 1:1.5 is quite satisfactory although a lower figure, down to 1:1.1 is desirable, but not very often achieved. If it is difficult to reduce the VSWR to below 2:1 then an antenna matcher may help.

What is an antenna matcher?

This is a small box with antenna input and output sockets (Fig. 17) containing a capacitive/inductive network which enables the

Fig. 17. A dual-control antenna matcher for 27 MHz. This is normally connected between the output of the transmitter and the antenna feed cable. The controls are adjusted until a low VSWR is obtained

antenna cable to be matched more accurately to the antenna. It should only be used in cases where the VSWR is higher than about 2:1, indicating an inadequate match to the antenna. It is sometimes called an 'antenna tuning unit' (ATU).

What is the purpose of a field strength meter?

This is basically a very simple receiver with usually no more than a small pick-up antenna, a tuned circuit, a rectifier diode and a meter. When in close proximity to an antenna that is being used for transmitting the field strength meter will show the relative strength of the radiation or field strength.

Are separate RF power meters available?

Some combined VSWR and power meters will give a reasonable indication of the power output from a CB transceiver but for really accurate measurements only a professional meter is capable of measuring power output very accurately and also power reflected from an antenna when this is not properly matched to the transceiver. This type of meter is necessary for measuring power and VSWR accurately at 934 MHz.

Is a dummy load an essential accessory?

Not essential but desirable, since a dummy load can be substituted for an antenna so that tests can be carried out on a transmitter without signals being radiated. A dummy load has a self-resistance exactly equal to the impedance required; for CB radio this is 50 ohms.

Are there problems with ignition interference to mobile operated equipment?

On 27 MHz a fairly high degree of ignition interference suppression may be necessary and there may also be interference from other electrical equipment. The most common type of interference is caused by spark plugs and the high voltage from the distributor. Nearly all modern vehicles use special high voltage anti-interference resistance cable to both plugs and the distributor unit. It may be necessary to fit suppressor capacitors to alternators or generators and also to voltage regulator devices. There is a possibility that noise energy from the ignition coil may find its way into the cable from the battery. This can be decoupled with a suitable coaxial capacitor. Electric motors for windscreen wipers and heater fans etc. may also have to be suppressed by decoupling with a suitable capacitor. Wheel static is a form of noise interference that can be produced by the spinning action of the wheels and a technique for eliminating this is the use of special 'static collector springs'. It is normal to have one fitted to each front wheel although sometimes static can be produced by the rear wheels as well. When a vehicle is in motion static can be produced by the tyres and this is particularly noticeable when the road is very dry. Kits are available from auto dealers containing a quantity of antistatic powdered carbon and a tool for injecting the powder into the tyre.

Adjoining sections of metal in a vehicle are not always in good electrical contact, which can create noise interference and poor contact is often due to corrosion or layers of paint. Bonding may be essential, consisting of straps of heavy copper braid which are used to join the separate sections of metal. One important place for bonding is between the engine block and the vehicle frame, particularly as the engine is often insulated from the frame. Ideally bonding should be made at several points. Complete suppression of noise due to vehicle electrics is often a job best carried out by specialist firms.

The 934 MHz band may not be so prone to ignition interference although special attention may be necessary to alternators and motor driven devices such as windscreen wipers.

Can microphones other those those supplied be used with a CB transceiver?

The press-to-talk method commonly used (the transmit button attached to the microphone) is not always convenient either when driving or even when operating a base station. Special microphones for mobile operation can be attached to a coat lapel, or clipped to a tie and headband types can hold the microphone in the right position for talking; either of these help to leave both hands free for driving. Most CB dealers have these types in stock and will advise or assist in re-connecting the microphone plug.

Desk type mics are more convenient for base station operation and these too are available from CB dealers. Again it may be necessary to change the connections at the microphone plug and no doubt dealers will also assist in this respect.

What type of antenna is necessary for either base station or mobile operation?

Only antennas that comply with the CB licence schedule may be used for CB in The UK. The subject of antennas is dealt with in Chapter 4.

What type of power supply is required to operate a mobile transceiver?

A typical well-designed power supply is shown in Fig. 18. The general requirement is that the supply is fully regulated and will deliver sufficient current to operate the transceiver when transmitting without the voltage output falling below 13 V. Most

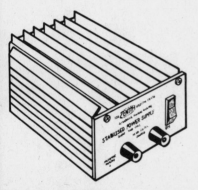

Fig. 18. A typical stabilised power supply for 13.8 V dc output with full regulation (see text)

power supplies are rated for 13.8 V at a specific current output which may be 3, 5, or 7 A. If the transceiver takes a total load on transmit of say 5 A then it would be better to use a supply rated for 7 A in which case the supply rail will maintain a steady 13.8 V. With poorly regulated power supplies the voltage will invariably drop to a very low level when the maximum current that the supply will deliver is exceeded even by a small margin.

4

Antennas and radio propagation at 27 MHz and 934 MHz

What are typical working ranges for CB radio?

CB radio is a short-range communication system and so the radio wave should be travelling mainly over a ground path (except for sky-wave propagation). Radio waves at 27 MHz suffer from ground-path attenuation and the strength rapidly diminishes as the distance increases. Since the effective radiated power allowed for 27 MHz is only 2 W the working ground range for CB radio may be more restricted than one might imagine. The average working range in daylight hours is little more than 13 to 16 km (8 to 10 miles). In very hilly country and in large and heavily built-up areas the range is considerably less. Mobile to mobile operation can have an even more restricted range partly due to the antenna on a vehicle roof not having the height for long-range work. With the approved 4 W of power reduced by the antenna to well under 2 W, mobile to mobile contacts are unlikely at ranges of more than 6 to 8 km (4 to 5 miles) even over relatively flat country. Signals are even more attenuated in very hilly and/or built-up areas. On 934 MHz the output power is 8 W and the type of antenna permitted may have an effective gain of about 5 dB, thus producing an effective radiated power of approximately 25 W, due to the directivity gain of the antenna. At these very high frequencies the mode of propagation is commonly referred to as 'line of sight'. Due to the natural curvature of the earth and certain conditions imposed by the lower atmosphere, the line of sight range is actually somewhat greater than would be a real visual line of sight distance. In open country ranges up to 24 km (about 15 miles) from base station to base station and up to 18 km (about 10 to 12 miles) from base station to mobile are possible. Working distances are much more severely restricted when propagation is either over very hilly country or through densely built-up areas, when range may be limited to little more than 2 to 5 km (1 to 3 miles).

However, further limitations on transmitted power are imposed by a Home Office ruling that if the antenna is higher than 7 metres for operation on 27 MHz and 10 metres for operation on 934 MHz, then the power from the transmitter must be reduced by 10 dB. This has the effect of reducing the working range already mentioned to a quarter or less.

What is ground-path attenuation?

As radio waves travel along the ground the power is absorbed more and more by the ground itself and after a given distance there is generally insufficient signal left that is capable of being detected by a receiver. Attenuation of this nature is highest at frequencies around 27 MHz.

What is sky-wave propagation?

At higher frequencies such as 27 MHz radio waves can leave the antenna at an angle to ground which is steep enough for the wave to travel upward. At a certain point in the earth's upper atmosphere waves propagating in this manner can be reflected downward again into areas several thousand kilometres from the point of origin. This mode of propagation is commonly referred to as 'long skip'. This applies particularly when the radio waves leave the antenna at angles in the region of 20° to 30°. Waves which travel upward at even steeper angles, e.g. in the region of 40° to 60° can also be reflected from the upper atmosphere and arrive at places between 150 and 1500 km (100 and 1000 miles) away, for example from the UK to France, Holland or Southern Italy. Radio

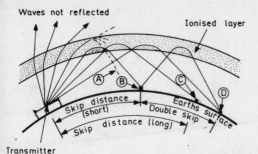

Waves not reflected

Ionised layer

(A) (B) (C) (D)

Skip distance (short)

Double skip

Skip distance (long)

Earths surface

Transmitter

Fig. 19. How radio waves are reflected from a part of the earth's upper atmosphere known as the ionised layer. The signal at (A) is only partially reflected. The signal arriving at (B) from the transmitter has made only a short skip whereas the signal arriving at (C) has made a single long skip. The signal arriving at (D) has reached this point by double skip, i.e. from transmitter to (B) and thence by reflection again to (D)

waves propagating in this way are doing so under a condition commonly known as 'short skip'. Fig. 19 illustrates how this takes place.

Is it possible to make contacts over very long distances?

This can often be accomplished because a region of the earth's upper atmosphere called the ionosphere has the property of reflecting radio waves. This region is sometimes referred to as the 'rarified atmosphere'. The amount of ultra-violet and other radiation from the sun has the effect of varying the height and the ionisation intensity of the ionospheric region. This effect becomes intensified approximately every eleven years and is due to, or coincides with, the appearance of large numbers of sunspots. It then becomes possible at various times to make contact on frequencies around 27 MHz with countries as far distant from the UK as America, Canada, Australia etc. Fig. 20 shows the time periods of maximum and minimum sunspot activity and it can be seen that the next period of maximum activity will occur around 1990. It is during the periods beginning just before and ending just after the maximum that the 'long skip' conditions prevail and when DX (long-distance) operation is at its best. 'Short skip' conditions are present almost continuously but are most effective during winter months, when they allow good contact with various European countries such as France, Italy and Holland etc.

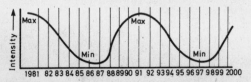

Fig. 20. *The rise and fall of sunspot activity between the years 1981 and 2000*

However, with the relatively low power and small antenna allowed for CB radio it may be difficult for European stations or indeed those at greater distances to hear very much of transmissions from the UK due to the very high power that is commonly used both in Europe and countries on the other side of the Atlantic. It is rather a case that you may hear them but they won't hear you.

What antennas may be used for CB radio on 27 MHz?

The specifications laid down by the Home Office for antennas to be used on 27 MHz has already been mentioned. In fact this is the only type of antenna that may be used legally and consists of a single section of radiating element not more than 1.5 metres long and with an inductance at the base to make the antenna resonant, i.e. tune to the frequency of operation and also provide a reasonable impedance match to the transceiver. This applies to antennas for both mobile and base station operation. Typical approved antennas for mobile operation are shown in Fig. 21. These antennas will only operate in conjunction with a 'ground

Fig. 21. These base loaded mobile antennas comply with the specification laid down by the Home Office for antennas to be used on 27 MHz (see text)

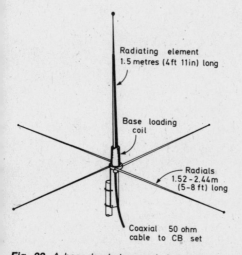

Radiating element
1.5 metres (4 ft 11 in) long

Base loading coil

Radials
1.52 - 2.44m
(5 - 8 ft) long

Coaxial 50 ohm cable to CB set

Fig. 22. A base loaded ground-plane antenna that meets the Home Office specification for CB radio on 27 MHz (see text)

plane', which for mobile operating is the body of the vehicle and which must, of course, be entirely metal. These antennas will not function with vehicles built of fibreglass. For base station operation the antenna is more or less the same but a proper ground plane must be provided which will normally be four or more horizontal conducting radial elements at the base of the antenna as shown in Fig. 22.

What antennas may be used for 934 MHz?

An antenna for this band may consist of up to four half-wavelength elements. The physical length at this frequency (of a

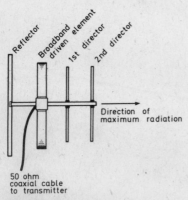

Fig. 23. A 4-element Yagi type antenna for 934 MHz. Such an antenna is directional and would need a rotator to ensure that radiation is transmitted in the desired direction and also to obtain the best reception

half-wavelength) is 160 mm. This allows a design capable of having 'directivity gain' which means that such an antenna will effectively radiate more power in a given direction. The antenna may be a small four-element Yagi type as shown in Fig. 23 but this has high directivity and therefore a rotator would be needed in order to transmit in any direction. It is possible to make an omnidirectional antenna, i.e. one which radiates equally in all directions, by arranging the elements one above the other, as shown in Fig. 24. This type of antenna is known as a 'colinear'.

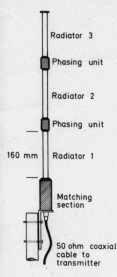

Radiator 3

Phasing unit

Radiator 2

Phasing unit

160 mm | Radiator 1

Matching section

50 ohm coaxial cable to transmitter

Fig. 24. A colinear antenna consisting of three stacked and phased dipoles for 934 MHz. Each radiator is driven in phase. This antenna could have four phased radiators to provide slightly more gain

With either type of antenna it is possible to achieve a directivity gain of 4 to 5 dB. This means that with an allowed transmitter power of 8 W such an antenna would have an effective radiated power in the region of 25 W. Such antennas call for precision construction and anything tht could be considered efficient could prove to be fairly expensive.

Does antenna height affect operating distance on 27 MHz?

It is a proven fact that the higher a transmitting antenna the greater is the range over which communications can be established along a ground path. However, the Home Office have effectively put a limit on the height at which antennas for both 27 MHz and 934 MHz may be used, since if the height of any 27 MHz antenna exceeds 7 metres above local ground level then the transmitting power must be reduced by 10 dB by means of the attenuator switch with which all approved CB transceivers must be fitted. In the case of 934 MHz the height limit is 10 metres, above which the power must be reduced by 10 dB.

How does antenna height affect operating distances on 934 MHz?

Provided the path of propagation is not unduly hilly or is over a densely built up area the working range on 934 MHz may well be

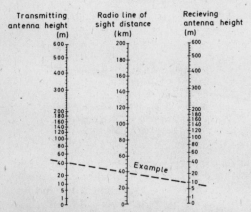

Fig. 25. Nomogram to determine range of radio signal for antenna height

beyond the real horizon or line of sight distance. However, the ranges of communication at frequencies in this region are at times greatly increased by certain tropospheric (lower atmosphere) conditions and contacts at up to 150 km (100 miles) or more are not unusual. Normal working ranges do depend a great deal on

60

the heights of the antenna used for transmitting and receiving. Generally speaking the greater the height the greater the distance worked. Fig. 25 gives some idea of the ranges possible with antennas at different heights (such as on tops of hills). However, remember the height limit of 10 metres for antennas operating on 934 MHz, and that if this height is exceeded the transmitting power must be reduced by 10 dB.

How efficient is the Home Office specified antenna for 27 MHz?

The efficiency of an antenna is determined largely by the amount of power it will radiate relative to the amount of power supplied to it. For example a dipole or half-wave antenna at 27 MHz is a fraction over 5 metres (17 feet) long and even allowing for the usual small resistive losses and ground losses that are associated with all antennas one would expect an efficiency of at least 90%, i.e. that 90% of the power supplied would be radiated. As the physical length of an antenna is reduced (relative to its natural length at resonance) so its ability to radiate efficiently is also reduced even though resonance is restored, as it must be, by inductive loading. The lower the efficiency the less power will be radiated and so the range of operation becomes less. It is, of course, possible to make a reasonably efficient shortened antenna by using centre inductive loading so as to produce half-wave resonance, but when an antenna for 27 MHz is reduced so much in order to meet the 1.5 metre limit imposed by the Home Office specification then the efficiency drops to a very low level, which in practice may be little more than 4 or 5%. Fig. 26 shows the average ranges possible with 27 MHz base station antennas of different design compared with the somewhat limited range that is imposed by the specified 1.5 metre base-loaded antenna. The tests involved in obtaining these measurements were carried out under virtually ideal conditions over flat countryside in normal daylight hours.

What is impedance?

All amplifiers that deliver power to a load must have an output resistance equivalent to the load resistance otherwise the available

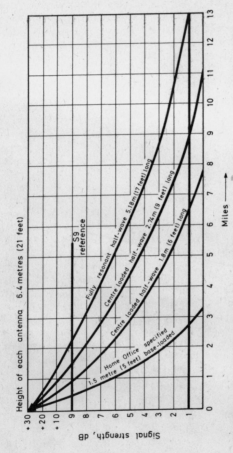

Fig. 26. The ranges obtained with three reasonably efficient 27 MHz antennas of different lengths as compared with the very short base-loaded antenna allowed by the Home Office for 27 MHz CB radio. The ranges shown are to a mobile receiver operating with a centre-loaded antenna. Power applied to each base-station antenna was 4 W and the height was set at 6.4 metres (21 feet) above ground (see text)

62

power may not all be transferred. However, when dealing with alternating power the output circuit resistance of the amplifier circuitry is referred to as 'impedance', a term which really means resistance to alternating voltage. This term is used for what is really the resistance to alternating voltage of the load itself. The output impedance common to all CB transceivers is 50 ohms, so any antenna which represents the load and is connected to the transmitter, must have the same impedance. This also applies to the transmission line or cable that is used to couple the transmitter to the antenna.

What is antenna tuning?

In order to operate efficiently the antenna must be tuned to the frequency of operation otherwise it will receive poorly and when used for transmitting some or even all the power supplied to it will be returned to the transmitter. This returned power is commonly called 'reflected power' and there is a definite relationship between this and the forward power, i.e. the power being supplied by the transmitter. Reflected power causes a standing wave to be set up along the feed cable between the transmitter and the antenna and it is the level of this standing wave that is measured when an antenna is being tuned. For this purpose a special meter is used to measure the *voltage standing wave ratio,* or VSWR, which is the ratio of the voltage generated by the forward power and the voltage generated by the reflected power.

What does a VSWR meter indicate?

The voltage standing wave ratio, or VSWR, is the ratio of the maximum and minimum voltage of a standing wave which is also equal to the ratio of the mismatch between the load impedance and the impedance of the transmitter output. If this were perfect then there would be no standing wave and the VSWR meter would read approximately 1 or what is normally termed a ratio of 1:1. However, if there is a mismatch then the VSWR is higher

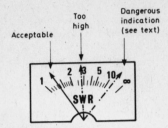

Fig. 27. *A VSWR reading of between 1 and 1.5 is about normal. Higher than 2 and approaching 3 is not acceptable. Above 10 and to infinity means an open or short circuit condition at the antenna or that the antenna is completely off tune. Avoid this condition always (see text)*

than 1:1 and can even reach infinity with an open or short circuit condition at either the transmitter or the antenna. This must always be avoided, as high levels of reflected power can seriously damage a transistorised transmitter output stage. An average VSWR reading would be between 1.1 and 1.5. Readings higher than 2:1 should be avoided (see Fig. 27).

How is an antenna fitted on a vehicle for mobile operation?

Apart from the necessary tuning to obtain a low VSWR reading there is little more work involved in fitting a mobile CB antenna than there is in fitting an ordinary car radio broadcast type antenna. However, virtually all mobile CB radio antennas are supplied with a special mounting socket or other base fitting and with instructions for installation. Coaxial type base sockets normally require that a hole is drilled though the vehicle body although some bases can be mounted on special brackets that will screw or clip onto the trunk (boot) lip or to the roof gutter. Some antennas can be used with a magnetic mount (mag-mount), a large cirular magnet with the built-in socket for the antenna, which will hold securely at the centre of a steel vehicle roof at normal road speeds. It is unwise to use antennas with magnetic mounts that are not really intended for this purpose as the wind resistance at high speed may pull the antenna and the magnetic mount from the roof. Some different mobile antenna mounts are shown in Fig. 28.

64

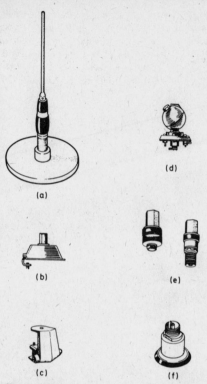

Fig. 28. Mobile antenna mountings: (a) magnetic, (b) trunk (boot) lip mount, (c) gutter mount, (d) ball type body mount, (e) standard ⅜th in socket body mounts SO239, (f) coaxial type body mount

Does the position of an antenna on a vehicle have any effect on its performance?

The ideal position for any mobile antenna whether for 27 MHz or 934 MHz is at the centre of the vehicle roof top where the largest area of ground plane is obtained. The radiation pattern of mobile antennas is affected somewhat when the antenna is mounted on either of the wing sides front or rear, although this is not as serious as one might think. The position of a mobile antenna is largely a matter of personal choice and with regard to any possible damage to the vehicle body caused by drilling holes in it.

Will mobile antennas operate on vehicle with fibreglass bodies?

The comments so far made with regard to mobile antennas apply to the specified base-loaded antenna and they will only operate on vehicles of all-metal construction. Base-loaded antennas will not operate on vehicles with fibreglass bodies unless some form of ground plane is provided, e.g. a large metal plate or radials mounted inside the roof of the vehicle. The base of the antenna, which is usually the braid or earth connection of the coaxial cable, must be connected to the ground plane. If in doubt, advice should be obtained from the antenna manufacturer. Certain types of centre-loaded antennas which are resonant to a half-wavelength will operate on fibreglass vehicles but they do not meet the Home Office specification.

How should a home (base) station antenna be installed?

Antennas for base station operation can be mounted separately on a free-standing mast, on a short mast attached to a chimney, or clamped to a brick wall at some convenient and accessible position (Fig. 29). Remember that the height of the antenna for 27 MHz must not exceed 7 metres (10 metres for 934 MHz) otherwise the power transmitted must be limited as already mentioned. As it is almost certain that adjustment will have to made to the antenna tuning for a low VSWR, it should be mounted so that it can be easily reached, as it is not normally possible to tune a transmitting antenna when it is on the ground. It is important to make sure that any antenna mounted on a mast or roof top is securely fitted and capable of withstanding the pressure of high wind. A typical installation is shown in Fig. 29c in which the ground plane antenna is mounted on a short stub mast attached to a chimney. Note how the cable is taken down and secured at intervals by wall clamps but note especially the 'drip loop' before the cable enters the house.

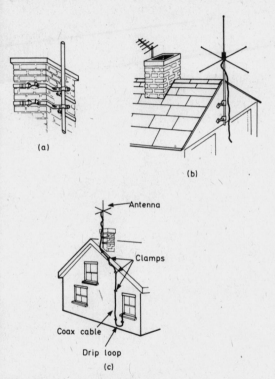

(a)

(b)

Antenna

Clamps

Coax cable

Drip loop

(c)

Fig. 29. (a) Chimney fittings for carrying a lightweight mast. (b) A base antenna can be mounted on a stub mast on an end wall. (c) How a cable run is made from the antenna down to the CB set. Note the loop at the bottom to allow water to drip off the cable

67

Is special cable necessary to connect the transmitter to the antenna?

The cable required is known as coaxial cable and for all CB equipment must have an impedance of 50 ohms. *Note:* television type coaxial cable must not be used as this has a higher impedance (75 ohms) and the screening braid is not suitable for transmitting use. Coaxial cable is available in several grades, some of which exhibit more attenuation (loss) then others per given length. The most common grade is RG58U or UR43 which is quite adequate for all mobile antenna installations and also base station installations where the cable run is not more than about 15 metres (50 feet). For longer cable runs a lower loss (larger) cable such as RG8U or UR67 should be used. Most CB

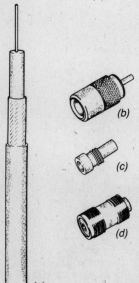

Fig. 30. (a) Standard solid dielectric 50 ohm coaxial cable. (b) Standard PL259 coaxial plug (sockets for these are standard on all CB equipment). (c) PL259 plug reducer for fitting and use of small diameter coaxial cable. (d) PL259 double socket coupler for joining two lengths of 50 ohm coaxial cable

Table 5. RG58 grades

Type	Nominal impedance (ohms)	Attenuation at 27 MHz (dB per 100 ft)	Power Handling at SWR 1:1 (Watts)	Comments
RG58	52	–	4256	Unspecified cable
RG58/U	53	1.9	430	Standard life – 5 yr
RG58B/U	53.5	1.9	430	Long life – 12 yr
RG58C/U	50	1.9	430	Long life – 12 yr

dealers have these cables in stock and will advise as to which may be best for your particular antenna installation. A section of single core solid dielectric 50 ohm coaxial cable with close meshed screening braid is shown in Fig. 30 and a summary of RG58 grade cables in Table 5.

5
Operating procedures

What callsigns are used for CB radio operation?

Callsigns similar to those issued to radio amateurs are not allocated by the Home Office for CB operation although some form of callsign, other than one's own name, is necessary for identification. The choice is entirely up to the operator. The custom generally is to make up a callsign, usually referred to as a 'handle', which is entirely a personal choice. For example there are purely descriptive names like Black Cat, Shaggy Dog, Silver Fox, or Black Knight etc. or the callsign can be related to where you live, for example, Riverman (who lives by the river), Marshman (who lives on the marshes), City Gent (who lives in the City). Lady CB operators can adopt feminine names such as Blondie, Redhead, Lady Bird etc. The choice is virtually unlimited, but obviously the use of any callsign that could be construed as obscene must not be used.

What does 'breaker' mean?

This is the general term used to describe a CB operator. It stems from the radio operating request to 'break in' which means to call straight in on a frequency channel otherwise used by other operators.

Are there specific calling channels for CB radio?

Generally the calling (breaking) channel in the UK is channel 14. Truck drivers and other mobile operators generally use channel 19 for calling. In some parts of the UK other channels are used for calling, either because of local difficulties or because the calling channels are so busy that another channel is used also. After making contact it is normal practice to move off the calling channel so that participants can continue their exchange of conversation on some other channel, thus leaving the calling channels clear for others.

How should a general call be made?

The procedure to establish a first contact is to set the transmitter on the appropriate calling channel. On channel 14 call as follows: *'One four for a copy, anyone for a copy'*, perhaps two or three times and then listen for a reply. If none is received, the call can be made again a short time later. The same applies when making a call on channel 19 in which case the call would be *'one nine for a copy'* etc. It is good practice to give your handle rather than the channel number when calling, then everyone knows who is calling. Anyone responding will know what channel number you are on, as otherwise they would not hear you.

How is your call acknowledged?

When another operator has heard your call, as above, the reply may be something like: *'breaker on the channel, this is . . ., what is your handle and what's your twenty'*. Note: 'handle' means callsign and 'twenty' (short for 10–20) means location. Your reply could be: *'Thanks for the call good buddy, this is . . . and my twenty is . . . Am receiving you nine pounds and ten four. Pick a window good buddy, come on back'*. 'Nine pounds' means a signal strength of S9. 'Ten four' (10–4) means 'message received'. 'Pick a window' means name another channel, 'Come on back' means 'Please reply'. Both operators then move to the agreed and hopefully unoccupied channel. *Note:* There are many small books available devoted to the jargon used in CB radio, most of which stems from America, where it was originaly used to pass information without the authorities understanding the message. However many UK operators feel that there is little point in using what to some seems a foreign language and that everyday conversational English is more desirable. Some abbreviations (e.g. the 10–code) are useful, but there is no real need to use jargon at all. However, many CB operators consider this all part of the fun of operating a citizen's band radio.

Is a channel reserved for emergency calls only?

The generally accepted channel for emergency calls only is channel 9. This is not normally used for general use, at least it should not be, but many CB operators listen continuously on this channel for any possible emergency call when they are not otherwise occupied on other channels. Some CB sets have automatic monitoring so that if you are listening on another channel any call that comes up on channel 9 is indicated by a light on the front of the set.

Is there a recommended code of practice for CB operation?

Yes; the following code was prepared after consultation with the Home Office by NATCOLCIBAR (National Committee for Leglisation of Citizens' Band Radio).

The conditions have deliberately been made simple with few restrictions. It is up to you to develop this service as you wish for the benefit of all. This means having consideration for one another and recognising that no-one has preferential rights at any time or place or on any channel. NATCOLCIBAR, the Parliamentary CB Working Party, and representatives of industry have in consultation with the Home Office prepared this simple code of practice. If you work to it you will help the system to help you.

HOW TO OPERATE

1. LISTEN BEFORE YOU TRANSMIT. Listen with the Squelch control turned fully down (and Tone Squelch turned off if you have Selective Call facilities) for several seconds, to ensure you will not be transmitting on top of an existing conversation.

2. KEEP CONVERSATIONS SHORT when the channels are busy, so that everyone has a fair share.

3. KEEP EACH TRANSMISSION SHORT and listen often for a reply – or you may find that the station you were talking to has moved out of range or that reception has changed for other reasons.

4. ALWAYS LEAVE A SHORT PAUSE BEFORE REPLYING so that other stations may join the conversation.

5. CB SLANG IS NOT NECESSARY – plain language is just as effective.

6. BE PATIENT WITH NEWCOMERS AND HELP THEM.

EMERGENCIES AND ASSISTANCE

7. AT ALL TIMES AND ON ALL CHANNELS GIVE PRIORITY TO CALLS FOR HELP.

8. LEAVE CHANNEL 9 CLEAR FOR EMERGENCIES. If you have to use it (for instance to contact a volunteer monitor service) get clear of it as soon as you can.

9. IF THERE IS NO ANSWER ON CHANNEL 9, then call for help on either channel 14 or 19, where you are likely to get an answer.

10. IF YOU HEAR A CALL FOR HELP, WAIT. If no regular volunteer monitor answers, then offer help if you can.

11. THERE IS NO OFFICAL ORGANISATION FOR MONITORING CB AND NO GUARANTEE THAT YOU WILL ALWAYS BE IN REACH OF A VOLUNTEER MONITOR.

CB IS *NOT* A SUBSTITUTE FOR THE 999 SERVICE.

CHOICE OF CHANNEL

12. RESPECT THE FOLLOWING CONVENTIONS:

Channel 9: Only for emergencies and assistance.
Channel 14: The calling channel. Once you have established a contact, move to another channel to hold your conversation.
Channel 19: For conversations among travellers on main roads. (Remember, if you are travelling in the same direction as the station you are talking to, not to hog this channel for a

long conversation). Give priority to the use of this channel by long distance drivers to whom it can be an important part of their way of life.

Other: You may find that particular groups in particular areas also have other preferred channels for particular purposes.

SAFETY

13. USE COMMONSENSE WHEN USING CB and do not transmit when it could be risky to do so. For example, do not transmit:

a. when fuel or any other explosive substance is in the open – e.g. at filling stations, when petrol or gas tankers are loading or unloading, on oil rigs, or at quarries.

b. when holding a microphone may interfere with your ability to drive safely.

c. with the antenna less than 150 mm (6 inches) from your face.

INTERFERENCE

14. INTERFERENCE can be caused by any form of radio transmission. Avoid the risks. Put your antenna as far away as possible from others, and remember that you are not allowed to use power amplifiers. In the unlikely event that your CB causes interference, cooperate in seeking a cure using the suggestions from a good CB handbook. Moving the set or antenna a short distance may cure the problem.

What is the 10 code?

This is a code originated, and still used, by the American State Police. A modified version of the code with different meanings has been devised solely for CB operators. The CB radio 10 code is generally as follows:

10–1	Receiving poorly	10–8	In service
10–2	Receiving well	10–9	Repeat message
10–3	Stop transmitting	10–10	Message completed – standing by
10–4	OK, message received	10–11	Talking too rapidly
10–5	Relay message	10–12	Visitors present
10–6	Busy, stand by	10–13	Advise road/weather conditions
10–7	Out of service		

10–16	Make pick up at . . .	10–50	Break channel
10–17	Urgent business	10–53	Road blocked
10–18	Anything for me	10–60	What is next message No.?
10–19	Nothing for you, return to base	10–62	Unable to copy use phone
10–20	My location is . . .	10–63	Write this down
10–21	Call by telephone	10–64	Network clear
10–22	Report in person to . . .	10–65	Awaiting your next message/assignment
10–23	Stand by	10–66	Cancel message
10–24	Assignment completed	10–67	All units comply
10–25	Get in touch with . . .	10–70	Fire at . . .
10–26	Disregard last message	10–71	Proceed with transmission in sequence
10–27	I am moving to channel . . .	10–73	Speed trap at . . .
10–28	Identify yourself	10–74	Negative
10–29	Time is up for contact	10–75	You are causing interference
10–31	Crime in progress	10–77	Negative contact
10–32	Radio check	10–81	Reserve hotel room for . . .
10–33	Emergency	10–84	My telephone No. is . . .
10–34	Help needed	10–85	My address is . . .
10–35	Confidential information	10–88	Advise telephone No. of . . .
10–36	Correct time is . . .	10–89	Radio repairman needed at . . .
10–37	Towtruck needed at . . .	10–90	I have TVI
10–38	Ambulance needed at . . .	10–91	Talk closer to mike
10–39	Your message delivered	10–92	Your transmitter is out of adjustment
10–41	Change to channel	10–93	Check my frequency
10–42	Traffic accident at . . .	10–94	Give me a long count
10–43	Traffic jam at . . .	10–95	Transmit dead carrier for 5 seconds
10–44	I have message for you	10–97	Check test signal
10–45	All units within range please report	10–99	Mission completed
10–46	Assist motorist	10–100	W.C./rest
		10–200	Police needed at . . .

Here are some examples of the use of the ten code:

'*You are 10–1*'. This means that the received signal is weak or poor quality. '*Give me a 10–9 on that good buddy*', sometimes just 'Ten-nine' or 'Nine?' This means 'Please repeat what you said'. '*Can you give me a 10–36*'. This means 'What is the correct time?' '*What is your 10–20?*' (usually abbreviated to 'What is your twenty?') means 'What is your location?'

What is the phonetic alphabet?

Phonetics are regularly used in radio communication and even in telephone communication in order to clarify the spelling of place names or vital words in messages. The commonly used phonetic alphabet is as follows and also includes phonetics for figures.

Letter	Phonetic Equivalent	Pronounced
A	ALPHA	Al Fah
B	BRAVO	Brah voh
C	CHARLIE	Char lee
D	DELTA	Dell ta
E	ECHO	Eck ho
F	FOXTROT	Foxs trot
G	GOLF	Golf
H	HOTEL	Hoh tell
I	INDIA	In dee ah
J	JULIET	Jew lee ett
K	KILO	Key loh
L	LIMA	Lee mah
M	MIKE	Mike
N	NOVEMBER	No vem bah
O	OSCAR	Oss cah
P	PAPA	Pap pah
Q	QUEBEC	Keh beck
R	ROMEO	Roh mee oh
S	SIERRA	See air rah
T	TANGO	Tang go
U	UNIFORM	Youu nee form

Letter	Phonetic Equivalent	Pronounced
V	VICTOR	Vik Tah
W	WHISKY	Wiss key
X	X-RAY	Ecks ray
Y	YANKEE	Yang key
Z	ZULU	Zoo Loo

0	ZERO		5	FI-YIV	
1	WUN		6	SIX	
2	TOO		7	SEV-EN	
3	THU-REE		8	ATE	
4	FOWER		9	NINER	

As an example the phonetic spelling of the word *'London'* would be Lima, Oscar, November, Delta, Oscar, November.

Is other special jargon used for CB radio?

Virtually all the jargon used for CB radio stems from American CB operators who conceived what is popularly known as 'Slanguage language'. Although its use is virtually unnecessary, because plain English is always more meaningful in any normal conversation, the following are some of the most used of the hundreds of different terms listed.

Ancient modulation – refers to AM or amplitude modulation
Antenna farm – a base station with a large array of different types of antennas
Armchair copy – receiving you as a very strong signal
Auntie Mary – AM
Back in a short short – will return to the channel in a few moments
Bare foot – operating legally with power acccording to the licence
Base station – a CB set installed at home or similar fixed location
Bears – the Police
Buzby – British Telecoms Radio Branch
Catch you later – signing off (or Down and Gone)
Channel hogger – CBer who talks too long
Chicken box – CB radio
Come back – please reply

Do you copy? – do you hear and understand me?

Down and on the side – finished talking but still listening

Ears – having the set on and receiving

Earwigging – listening to other CBer's conversations

Eyeball – meeting another CBer in person ('eyeball to eyeball')

Getting out – you are being heard, good clear reception

Going down – signing off

Got your ears on? – are you listening?

Good numbers – best wishes

Home twenty – location of base station or own residence

I'm through – sign off, finish transmitting

In the clear – no interference on your signals

Jammed out – blocked out by interference

Juice – petrol or other motor fuel

Keying the mic – transmitting without speaking

Landline – telephone

Lid – a poor operator

Motion lotion – motor fuel

Negative copy – unable to understand your transmission

Negatory – no

On standby – listening but not transmitting

On the side – standby and listening

Pass the numbers to you – best wishes

Pick a clean one – select another channel

Pick a window – choose a channel

QSL card – postcard sent to confirm CB contact

Quickie – a short conversation

Ratchet – talk on CB radio

Ratchet jaw – a CBer who hogs the channel and talks too much

Radio (or Rig) check – give me a report on my transmission

Rig – CB radio

Running a boot – using a linear amplifier

Salt mine – place of employment

Say again – repeat your transmission

Seventy-three – best wishes

Skip – signals from great distance

Smokey – the Police

SWR – sometimes referred to as 'SWER' means standing wave ratio

Ten-four – message received

That's a copy – I read you clearly

VOX – voice operated relay. Automatically switches on transmitter when operator speaks into the microphone

Walked all over – overpowered by a stronger signal
Walkie-talkie – portable CB transceiver
Wall to wall – very strong received signal
XYL – The wife
Yogi bear – Police
YL – young lady
Zeds – sleeping

There are so many terms and phrases that one booklet published contains some 2500 entries.

What other operating codes may be used?

Some CB operators use the RST code and the Q code, both of which are commonly used by radio amateurs.

THE RST CODE

Readibility
R1   Unreadable
R2   Barely readable
R3   Readable with difficulty
R4   Readable with practically no difficulty
R5   Perfectly readable

Strength (signal)
S1   Faint signals, barely perceptible
S2   Very weak signals
S3   Weak signals
S4   Fair signals
S5   Fairly good signals
S6   Good signals
S7   Moderately strong signals
S8   Strong signals
S9   Extremely strong signals

Tone (refers to quality of morse code signals)
T1   Extremely rough tone
T2   Very rough tone
T3   Rough tone
T4   Rather rough but better than T3

T5	Reasonably clean tone
T6	Clean tone
T7	Nearly d.c. tone i.e., a little mains hum audible
T8	Good d.c. tone, slight trace of hum
T9	Pure tone
T9X	Indicates clear crystal controlled transmission

Example: 'Your signals are 5 and 9', meaning R5 (perfectly readable) and S9 (extremely strong signals). The tone code is only used if transmissions are in morse code.

THE 'Q' CODE

Signal	Question	Reply
*QRA	What **station** are you?	I am **station** _____.
QRB	How **far** are you from me?	I am _____ miles away.
	Where are you **headed** and from where?	I am bound for _____ from _____.
	What is your estimated **time of arrival** at ____ ?	I expect to arrive in ____ at _____.
QRF	Are you **returning** to ____ ?	I am returning to _____.
*QRG	What is my exact **frequency**?	Your frequency is _____.
*QRK	How do you read my **signals**?	Your signals are _____. (1) Unreadable (2) Readable now and then (3) Readable with difficulty (4) Readable (5) Perfectly readable
*QRL	Are you **busy**?	I am busy.
*QRM	Are you experiencing **interference**?	I am experiencing interference.
*QRN	Are you troubled by **static**?	I am troubled by static.
*QRT	Shall I **stop** transmitting?	Stop transmitting.
*QRU	Have you **anything** for me?	I have nothing for you.
QRV	Are you **ready**?	I am ready.

Signal	Question	Reply
*QSA	What is the strength of my signals?	Your signals are _____ (1) Scarcely perceptible (2) Weak (3) Fairly good (4) Good (5) Very good
*QSB	Are my signals **fading**?	Your signals are fading.
*QSL	Will you send me a **confirmation** of our communication?	I will confirm.
QSM	Shall I **repeat** the last message?	Reapeat the last message.
*QSO	Can you **communicate** with _____ ?	I can communicate with .
QTC	How many **messages** do you have for me?	I have _____ messages for you.
*QTH	What is your **location**?	I am at _____.
QTN	At what **time** did you **depart** from _____ ?	I left _____ at _____.
QTO	Have you **left port** (dock)?	I have left port (dock).
QTP	Are you going to **enter port** (dock)?	I am going to enter port (dock).
*QTR	What is the correct **time**?	The correct time is _____.
QTU	During what **hours** is your station open?	My station is open from _____ to _____.
QTV	Shall I **stand guard** for you on ___ MHz/kHz?	Stand guard for me on _____ MHz/kHz.
QTX	Will you keep your station open for **further communication** with me for _____ hours?	I will keep my station open for further communication with you for _____ hours.
QUA	Do you have **news** of ___ ?	Here is news of _____.

Those marked thus * are fairly regularly used by radio amateurs and are being adopted by CB operators.

What is REACT?

This is a volunteer organisation whose members permanently monitor channel 9, internationally recognised as the channel for emergency communications. REACT (Radio Emergency Associated Citizens' Teams) was founded in the USA in 1962. In the UK the organisation is known as REACT ALERT which stands for React Action League of Emergency Radio Teams. The objectives of REACT ALERT are to assist in all forms of local emergencies by furnishing instant radio telephone communications in cooperation with proper authorities and official agencies; to maintain and encourage operating efficiency and to operate and maintain equipment at peak efficiency and in accordance with Home Office regulations. The main aim is of course to promote the proper and effective use of the official emergency CB channel.

Fig. 31. *The badge of the REACT emergency CB radio communication service*

REACT also plan to develop a 24-hour monitoring service for emergency calls and to coordinate their efforts with other groups such as the British Red Cross, St. John's Ambulance and local and national authorities in cases of emergency and disaster. Those interested in the activity of REACT should contact REACT ALERT, Dolphin House, Williams Avenue, Wyke Regis, Weymouth, Dorset. The official badge of REACT is shown in Fig. 31.

Are there any other emergency organisations?

Some counties in the UK have emergency radio systems in which CB operators may participate. Others may well follow but details of existing organisations can be obtained by writing to any of the regular monthly CB radio magazines.

Table 6. Table of country specifications

	France	Germany Holland	Norway	Denmark	Spain	Italy	Sweden	USA	UK
Number of channels	22	22	22	23	10	Anything goes!	24	40	40
Frequency	26.960 27.230	26.960 27.230	26.960 27.230	26.960 27.230	27.035 27.205		26.960 27.260	26.965 27.405	27.6025 27.99125
Spacing (kHz)	10	10	10	10	10		10	10	10
Max. RF power (W)	2	0.5	0.5	0.5	0.5		3.5	4	4
Max. radiated power (W)	0.4	0.1	0.1	0.1	0.1		0.7	4	2
Modulation	FM	FM	AM FM SSB	AM FM	AM FM		AM FM SSB	AM SSB	FM

84

Can CB radio be used on public transport?

There is no ruling in the CB licence that prohibits the use of CB radio on public transport, e.g. buses and trains although CB radio must not be used on any aircraft. However, public transport companies may have their own byelaws concerning this and one would be well advised to check before actually transmitting from a public vehicle and especially on railway trains as some railway systems employ VHF communications to which the use of CB equipment might cause serious interference.

Is it possible to contact CB stations in other countries?

There is nothing to prevent CB operators from making contact with CB stations in other countries provided an approved antenna is used and the power limit is not exceeded. However, contact is unlikely with other countries as most of them are using a different frequency range to the UK and have a lower power limit (see Table 6). At times American and Italians can be heard due to skip, but it is extremely unlikely that they will be able to hear you.

Is it worthwhile keeping a station log book?

All licensed radio amateurs must keep a log book listing callsigns of the contacts they make, the frequency of operation and times and dates of contacts etc. Many regard this as a valuable record and also include notes about radio conditions prevailing at the time, the antenna and equipment that was being used, weather conditions, etc. details of these all being entered in the log at the time of making contact. Many CB operators also find that keeping a log book is worthwhile and useful to refer to should it be necessary to confirm that your station was, or was not, operating at a certain time and on a certain date should a complaint of interference be received. Details kept in a log book

Date	Station called	Called by station	Location of station	Time started	Time concluded	Subject discussed	Channel number

Fig. 32. Recommended layout for a CB radio log book. Printed log books with similar layouts are available

are useful for the information required when making an exchange of QSL cards, i.e. cards confirming contacts between two stations. A suggested layout for a station log book is shown in Fig. 32.

What are QSL cards?

The code letters QSL mean *acknowledgment of receipt of your message*. Radio amateurs use QSL cards extensively to acknowledge contacts made with each other and it is a time honoured custom with many to decorate the walls of their stations with hese cards, especially those confirming long distance contacts, or example with Australia, New Zealand, South America etc. The cards are useful as proof of contact with various countries to obtain certificates of merit issued by clubs or societies. The QSL card is usually postcard size and carries the station callsign and address, as well as spaces for noting the channel and frequency used, time and date of contact and usually information about the equipment and antenna used etc. Printers of QSL cards will be found advertising in most of the monthly CB magazines and they are always pleased to send samples of standard designs or will print cards to your own special design.

How are QSL cards exchanged?

This can either be done directly by post provided you have the name and address of your contact, or through organised QSL exchange bureaux run for CB operators in most countries. Any local club or society or one of the regular CB magazines will be able to give information.

Should one be insured against theft of equipment and/or damage caused by a falling antenna?

Yes, it is a good idea and some insurance companies specialise in providing insurance against the theft of CB and other radio equipment from cars or from the home; many advertise in the various monthly CB radio magazines. Insurance can be taken out to cover damage caused by an antenna falling on your own or other people's property and also causing personal injury. Advice here is to consult your own insurance company or broker.

Should precautions be taken against lightning strikes in stormy weather?

While it is possible to fit lightning arresters in the coaxial cable where it plugs into the CB set, by far the safest method of avoiding damage to the transmitter from lightning strikes, is to disconnect the coaxial cable from the set and leave it disconnected until the storm has passed. Short circuit the plug with a screw-driver afterward to discharge any static build up that may have occurred in the cable before re-connecting it to the transmitter. The best place for a lightning arrester is in the cable where it leaves the mast. It should be properly earthed with a substantial earth wire to a metal ground stake or plate.

Is it dangerous to transmit from a vehicle whilst the petrol tank is being filled?

Yes in no circumstances should a CB set be switched to transmit whilst petrol is being taken on. Petrol filling pipes and pumps are usually grounded. The CB transmitter and the antenna on a vehicle are well insulated from the ground on rubber tyres, and can therefore be at high RF potential if the transmitter is switched on. Contact between the vehicle body and the metal petrol filler pipe can cause a spark because the pipe will try to discharge the RF potential to ground. It requires only a small spark to ignite the fumes that surround a petrol tank when filling is taking place. To be really safe a CB transmitter should be switched off completely whilst filling up with petrol.

What are the common causes of interference to other services due to CB radio?

The most common form of interference attributable to CB radio is breakthrough of the transmitter carrier into television receiver circuitry which can cause the pictures to become extremely distorted or the voice of the CB operator to appear on the TV sound channel. Carrier breakthrough into the circuitry of conventional transistor radio sets or hi-fi systems is also quite common and here the effect is either severe distortion of the sound that one is listening to, or the voice of the CB operator being superimposed upon the reproduction. Interference can also be caused to other services by harmonics directly related to the fundamental frequency on which the CB transmitter is operating. These harmonics can occur on frequencies that are the same as the normal frequencies being used by some other service such as Police radio, ambulance and fire service communications, business radio and marine radio communications systems, etc. that nearly all operate on VHF (very high frequencies).

What can be done if my CB reception is spoiled by interference from other radio services?

Again CB operators have no priority but if the cause of interference is known it may be possible to come to some form of agreement with the owners of the interfering equipment to effect a satisfactory cure, possibly with the assistance of the British Telecom radio interference branch.

What are common causes of interference to CB radio by other services?

If you are located very close to a transmitter operated by official services, or one used for radio or television broadcasting, interference from either might well be expected, but there are possible cures for this. Interference can also be caused to CB radio reception by cetain types of equipment that generate high frequency power, e.g., hospital diathermy machines and radio frequency plastic welding systems. Noise interference is usually caused by unsuppressed electric motors, thermostats, electric welding equipment and fluorescent and neon type lighting.

What is necessary to prevent my CB set from causing interference to other services?

The common causes of interference by CB radio to other services have been dealt with in previous questions. Prevention can be difficult, generally involving special filters being fitted either to your own equipment, or to the equipment to which interference is being caused, hence the reason for the advice previously given about getting expert help. It may not be a simple matter of connecting a ready made so-called TVI filter to your CB set, or neighbour's TV set. Specially designed filters can sometimes effect a cure, but not always. Tampering with your own or someone else's equipment could do more harm than good. Other CB operators and even CB dealers are not always knowledgeable enough to give proper advice concerning suitable filters etc., or even reasons why interference is being caused in the first instance. If your CB set is known to be causing interference to any other service the only people that can give accurate advice are British Telecoms radio interference branch.

Remember that your licence says that your set should not cause undue interference – if it does, you should solve the problem as soon as possible.

6
Glossary of technical terms

Many of the technical terms found in publications concerned with CB radio may seem strange to the newcomer. The following are some of the terms including brief explanations.

Amplitude Modulation (AM) The modulation of a sine wave carrier by a fluctuating audio signal so that its amplitude varies in sympathy with the signal.

Angle Modulation Modulation in which the electrical angle of a carrier wave is varied by the modulating signal. This includes *frequency modulation* and *phase modulation*.

Antenna A rod used to radiate radio waves and to receive incoming radio waves. An assembly of antennas that have directional characteristics is known as an *antenna array*.

Antenna Matching Unit A capacitive inductive circuit used to match the impedance of an antenna to either a receiver or transmitter, or both.

Attenuation A decrease in the amplitude of any audio or radio signal either through transmission lines or over a (radio) transmission path. Usually expressed as a ratio in decibels.

Audio Frequency (AF) Any frequency at which a sound wave becomes audible to the human ear. The generally accepted range is from about 15 Hz to 20 kHz.

Automatic Frequency Control (AFC) A system designed to keep a receiver exactly in tune to a wanted station. If the receiver is mistuned a control voltage is generated which is used to adjust the frequency of the local oscillator to bring the receiver back into tune.

Automatic Gain Control (AGC)   Sometimes known as automatic volume control, a system intended to produce a near-constant level of signal over a specified range of variation in signal level.

Balun   Derived from the term 'balance-to-unbalance', a device used to couple a balanced antenna such as a dipole to an unbalanced (coaxial) transmission line.

Beam Width   Refers to the width of the main lobe produced by a beam antenna. The main lobe width, usually measured in degrees, is taken at a point where the radiation is 3 dB down from absolute maximum.

Beat Frequency Oscillator (BFO)   A variable frequency oscillator, the signal from which can be mixed into the final intermediate frequency amplifier to produce an audible tone when the receiver is tuned to a CW signal, i.e. morse transmission

Callsign   A combination of letters and figures or a specific name used by stations to identify themselves during transmission.

Capture Effect   The suppression of a weak signal by a much stronger signal on the same frequency; applies in frequency modulation reception.

Carrier Wave   The wave transmitted from a radio station which is fundamentally a continuous sine wave at the frequency of transmission.

Channel   A specific frequency used for transmission. A frequency band may be divided into a number of separate channels each having its own frequency.

Characteristic Impedance   The real impedance of a transmission line or an antenna, or applies to any electrical circuit having a specific input or output impedance.

Citizen's Band Radio   A short-range radio service intended for use by unqualified operators. No technical examination is required for a licence.

Clipping   Distortion that occurs to an electrical signal produced by an amplifier which is unable to cope with the peaks of the input signal.

92

Coaxial Cable   A transmission line which consists of two conductors one inner and one outer both being insulated from each other.

Colinear   An antenna consisting of multiple radiating elements coupled so that each one operates in phase with the others.

Cross Modulation   May occur if a strong unwanted signal causes overloading at the input of a receiver. The unwanted station will be heard as a background to the wanted signal.

Decibels (dB)   A logarithmic unit used to express the ratio of two values of either electrical power, voltage or current. The decibel is commonly used for expressing gain or loss in any form of transmission or amplifying system.

Demodulation   The process of extracting the original information from a modulated radio signal. The device used for this is usually called a *demodulator* or *detector*.

Desensitising   A reduction in sensitivity of a radio receiver when a very strong signal is present on any of its range of channels, not necessarily the one it is tuned to receive.

Deviation   The change in frequency of a carrier wave when it is angle modulated or frequency modulated.

Dipole   A balanced antenna system with a physical length equal to one half wavelength at the frequency of operation.

Direct Current (DC)   Current flowing in one direction only which does not change its polarity.

Direction Finding (DF)   A method of determining the position of a transmitter by using a radio receiver coupled to a special directional antenna.

Distortion   The malformation of an otherwise perfect waveform due to non-linearity in an amplifying system or non-linearity in the frequency response of an amplifying system.

Double Sideband (DSB)   When both sidebands are produced during the process of amplitude modulation and are transmitted at the same level of power.

Driven Element   Any element in an antenna system that is directly energised by power from the transmitter.

Dummy Load   A purely resistive device which may be substituted for the normal load on a transmitter output, e.g. an antenna.

DX   Long distance communication.

E-layer   A layer of intense ionisation that occurs at approximately 100 km above the surface of the earth. At night the density decreases.

Earth   The term usually applied to the earth as a conductor of electricity or as that part of any electrical circuit which is at zero potential. The term 'ground' is sometimes used instead of earth, e.g. as in *ground plane.*

Effective Radiated Power (ERP)   Usually, the power radiated by an antenna. It can be greater than or less than the power supplied depending on whether the antenna is directional and has gain or has a low efficiency when compared with a reference antenna.

Electromagnetic Wave   Radio waves or light waves, the product of the electric and magnetic fields that are generated.

Electromotive Force (EMF)   The electrical force produced by a battery or generator which causes a flow of current through any externally connected circuit.

F-layer   Two separate ionised layers known as F1 and F2 which exist separately during daylight hours and combine at night to form one layer. They refract radio waves.

Fading   Variations in the strength of radio signals which may be due to propagation conditons.

Feeder   Another term for *transmission line,* used for the connection of an antenna to a transmitter or receiver.

Field Strength   The amplitude of the electric field produced by a radiated wave.

Field Strength Meter   An instrument for giving a direct reading of the field strength of a radio wave.

Free Space Antenna   An antenna such as the dipole that operates without being greatly affected by the presence of the ground beneath it.

Frequency Modulation (FM)   A form of modulation which alters the frequency of the radio carrier in sympathy with the amplitude of the modulating (audio) signal.

Frequency Response   The response of an amplifier or other electrical circuit to a wide range of frequencies or changes in frequency.

Fundamental Frequency The lowest frequency present in a complex wave which might contain other and higher frequencies. Can also apply to the working frequency of a transmitter.

Ground-plane Antenna An antenna system which employs an artificial ground in the form of a number of conducting radials connected to the base.

Ground Wave A transmitted radio wave that travels along the surface of the earth. Sometimes known as a *surface wave*.

Harmonic One of the components of a fundamental wave but which occurs at a frequency of twice, or three, or four times, or greater than the fundamental frequency.

Helically Wound Antenna An antenna in which the whole of the conductor is spirally wound onto an insulating support.

Hertz (Hz) The unit of frequency and equal to cycles per second.

High-pass Filter A frequency selective network that attenuates lower frequencies and passes high frequencies above a defined point.

Impedance The equivalent of resistance in circuits carrying an alternating current or voltage comprising the combination of the reactive and purely resistive components in the circuit.

Integrated Circuit (IC) A device containing a number of transistors, diodes, resistors and capacitors and all the necessary connections to make a complete circuit.

Interference Term used when an unwanted signal occurs at a level high enough to spoil the reception of a wanted signal.

Intermediate Frequency (IF) The frequency which is produced by mixing the frequency of the incoming signal and that of a local oscillator. This frequency is then further amplified and finally drives the demodulating stage in a complete receiver.

Ionosphere A part of the earth's atmosphere in which the propagation of radio waves is affected by ionisation due to the sun's rays.

Linear Amplifier A radio frequency amplifier in which the output rises linearly as the signal to its input is increased. Not permitted for use with CB radio equipment.

Local Oscillator (LO) An oscillator from which the output frequency is mixed with the frequency of signals being received.

Either the sum or difference frequency that is produced by this is used as the intermediate frequency of the receiver.

Lower Sideband (LSB) The sideband that contains all the frequencies below a carrier frequency which has been amplitude modulated.

Low-pass Filter A frequency selective network used to pass low frequencies below a certain point and attenuate all high frequencies above that point.

Modulation The superimposing of a signal on a continuous wave, i.e. a carrier wave, so that the wave itself varies according to the amplitude of the modulating signal.

Muting Cutting off the high noise level normally produced by an FM receiver in the absence of any received signal.

Omnidirectional Antenna An antenna which radiates equally in all directions around it in either a vertical or horizontal plane. Commonly applies to all vertical antennas.

Oscillator A circuit which may use a transistor or valve for the generation of alternating signals at virtually any frequency from sub-audio to ultra-high frequencies as used in radio transmission.

Phase Lock Loop (PLL) An integrated circuit that produces an output voltage with polarity and level proportional to the phase difference between two input signals.

Polar Diagram A form of graph using polar coordinates for showing the radiation from an antenna in one plane or another.

Polarisation A property determined by the direction of the electric field produced by an antenna. Vertical antennas for example radiate vertically polarised waves.

Power Amplifier Usually the final amplifier stage of an audio or radio frequency system which supplies power to the load and which may be a loudspeaker in the case of audio, or an antenna in the case of radio.

Push-to-Talk (PTT) Switch A press switch usually attached to the microphone for switching the transmitter on. Commonly used on all CB transceiver microphones.

Radiation Pattern A graph, usually in polar coordinate form, for showing the level of radiation from an antenna at all angles around it.

Radio Frequency   Any frequency above the audio and super-sonic range, i.e. above 100 000 Hz. The radio-frequency spectrum then extends into a range covering thousands of millions of Hz, being segregated into specific bands such as low, medium, high, ultra-high and super-high frequencies.

Resonance   The condition of a tuned circuit, or an antenna, when the capacitive reactance is balanced out by the inductive reactance. Resonance occurs only a a single frequency.

'S' Meter   A meter calibrated in figures from one to nine to indicate the relative levels of received radio signals.

Selectivity   The ability of a receiver to differentiate between a wanted signal on one particular frequency and unwanted signals on frequencies in close proximity.

Sensitivity   The ability of a receiver to respond to weak signals and still produce a readable received signal.

Signal-to-Noise Ratio   The ratio of the amplitude of a signal to the amplitude of noise, the ratio usually being expressed in decibels.

Single Sideband (SSB)   A mode of operation in which either the upper sideband or lower sideband of an amplitude modulated wave is transmitted. The unwanted sideband is filtered out.

Skip Distance   The distance in a given direction from a transmitter where reception by ionospheric reflection is possible.

Space Wave   A radio wave that travels directly from a transmitting antenna to a receiving antenna.

Standing Wave   The field pattern created by two waves of the same frequency being propagated in different directions along a transmission line.

Standing Wave Ratio   The full term is *voltage standing wave ratio,* which means the amplitude of reflected voltage as a ratio of the amplitude of the forward voltage being supplied to an antenna.

Television Interference (TVI)   Refers to interference to domestic television reception caused by a radio transmitter operating on some other frequency.

Transceiver   A unit which combines both the transmitter and receiver. Most CB sets are of the transceiver type, some being completely self-contained with a mains power supply.

Transmission Line A special line or cable for conveying radio frequency power from a transmitter to an antenna. The common type of line used for CB radio is known as a *coaxial line* or *cable*.

Troposphere (Tropospheric) The lower portion of the earth's atmosphere through which very high frequency radio waves will travel without too much attenuation. Certain tropospheric conditions can arise that extend the normal working range at VHF from a few miles to hundreds of miles. For CB radio these conditions would only affect the 934 MHz band.

Ultra-High Frequency (UHF) Refers to frequencies above about 300 MHz and up to about 1000 MHz.

Upper Sideband (USB) The sideband containing all the modulation signals which is above the nominal frequency of the carrier.

Variable Frequency Oscillator (VFO) A highly stable oscillator but which can be varied in frequency. Normally used as the master oscillator of a transmitter.

Very-High Frequency (VHF) This refers to frequencies in the range between 30 MHz and 300 MHz.

Voltage Controlled Oscillator (VCO) Usually a highly stable oscillator used in transmitters but the frequency can be varied by an external controlling voltage.

Voice Operated Transmitting (VOX) A system that automatically switches the transmitter on when the operator speaks into the microphone. Sometimes referred to as *voice operated carrier*.

VSWR See *Standing Wave Ratio*.

Waveband A band of wavelengths or frequencies allocated for a given communication service, for example, the 27 MHz CB radio waveband extends from 27.60125 to 27.99125 MHz.

Wavelength Normally the distance in metres between the peaks of a wave at a given frequency. For example at a frequency of 27 MHz the wavelength is approximately 11.1 metres.

Whip Antenna A vertical flexible antenna usually with inductive loading to make it resonant at the frequency of operation. Type of antenna popularly used for mobile operation.

Yagi Antenna   A special directional antenna normally consisting of a single driven element and a number of parasitic elements, one usually being a reflector, the remainder being known as directors.

Index

Accessories, 46
AM to FM conversion, 25
Amateur radio, 8
Amplitude modulation, 15
Angle modulation, 15
Antenna
  efficiency, 61
  height, 59, 60
  matcher, 48
  tuning, 63
Antennas
  general, 53
  home-base, 68
  indoor, 45
  mobile, 64
  27 MHz, 56
  934 Mhz, 58

BCI (broadcast interference), 29
Boats, 26, 37
Books, 10
Breaker, 71
Buying a CB set, 27

Calling, 72
Calling channels, 71, 72
Calls, emergency, 1, 73
Callsigns, 8
Capture effect, 18
Causes of interference, 88
Channel numbers, 20

Coaxial cable, 68
Codes
  Q code, 81
  RST code, 81
  ten code, 78
Code of practice, 73
Conversion units, 40
Cross modulation, 30

Dangerous practice, 88
Decibels, 30
Decibel table, 31
Deviation, 17
Dummy load, 30, 49

EIA standard, 27
Effective radiated power, 19
Eleven year cycle, 56
Emergency organisations, 82, 83
Emergency use, 1, 73
Equipment, 3, 34
Equipment test reports, 27

Fibreglass vehicles (antennas), 67
Field strength meter, 48
Filtrers, 30
Frequency modulation, 15
Frequencies of operation, 13, 14

Glossary, 91
Ground-path attenuation, 54
Ground-plane antennas, 56, 57, 58

Handheld CB sets, 42
Harmonic radiation, 28
High pass filters, 30, 32
Home base station antennas, 68
Home base station installation, 42
Home built sets, 40
Home Office specifications, 12

Ignition interference, 49
Illegal equipment, 41
Impedance, 61, 63
Indoor antennas, 45
Insuring equipment, 87

Jargon, 78, 80

Linear amplifier, 28
Log books, 85
Long distance contacts, 55
Low pass filter, 30, 44

Microphones, 50
Mobile operation, 64
Mobile set installation, 35, 36
Modifications, 41
Mountings
   base antenna, 67
   mobile antenna, 65

Natcolcibar, 73

Operating bands, 3
Operating procedure (general), 71
Other countries, 85

PA facility, 22
Performance specifications, 38, 39
Phase modulation, 15
Phonetic alphabet, 77
Power supplies, 24, 51
Public transport, 55,

Push-to-talk (PTT), 22

'Q' code, 81
QSL cards, 86

Radiation danger, 934 MHz, 32
Range of sets to choose from, 37
REACT, 82
Repairs, 42
Restrictions, 6
RF power meters, 49
RST code, 80

Scanner receivers, 26
Selcal (selective calling), 33
Selectivity (receivers), 28
Sensitivity (receivers), 28
Setting up a CB station, 9
Sideband modulation, 16
Sideband splatter, 17
Signal strength, 18
Sky-wave propagation, 54
Speech processing, 24, 41
'S' meter, 18
SWR, 46, 47, 64

Technical terms (glossary), 91
Telephone to CB links, 25
Ten code, 75
Transmitter power, 19
Transistors on CB sets, 27
TVI (television interference), 29

UK CB bands, 11
Users, CB, 2, 4

VOX (voice operated control), 32
VSWR, 46, 47, 64

Weather (storm) precautions, 87
Working ranges, 53, 62